A "must-read" for local or regional food companies looking to get on – and stay on – the retail shelf and maximize the value of their brand."
Edward Reidy, President Happy Apples

Moving Your Brand Up the Food Chain™

Marketing Strategies to Grow Local & Regional Food Brands

By Patrick Nycz

"Natural, organic, local, sustainable, craft, artisan – the market for food is exciting and dynamic – and the market is open to food entrepreneurs with exciting new products/concepts. But, building a local or regional food brand and carving out space in the food store and food service market is a daunting task for anyone, let alone an entrepreneur/small company.

In *Moving your Brand up the Food Chain*, Patrick Nycz has pulled back the curtain on building an exciting and profitable food brand. Loaded with original research and case examples, Nycz takes the food entrepreneur/regional food company through every step of the brand building process in a pragmatic, focused way. (Not to be missed is Chapter 3, *The Buyer Perspective*, where results of extensive interviews with food buyers/retailers provide deep insights into what it takes for a new food product/company to be successful with their organizations). If you are ready to take your food product from the farmer's market or CSA to the food store, or ready to take your local brand to regional/national distribution, this book is for you."

Jay Akridge, Glenn W. Sample Dean of Agriculture, Purdue University

"I've seen the principles in this book in action! There is no question the marketing strategies Patrick and NewPoint has guided us through work and have been a big part of growing our Indiana Kitchen brand over the past decade."

Russell L Yearwood, President, Indiana Packers Corp.

"Through this book, Patrick presents a systematic process that really helps you focus on what's important for the success of your products and brand allowing you to avoid costly and brand-killing trial and error. Everyone knows it's important to stand out but you must get on the retail shelf first. This book will guide there and maximize the value of your brand."

Edward Reidy, President Happy Apples

Even after working and being so familiar with Patrick and his marketing team for more than 30 years, it's still fascinating to see their principles outlined so clearly in this book. It's like the reverse of applied learning, and it only validates how they have a unique ability to know your business so well, and still surprise you with new ideas. Without question, for anyone in the food-industry who is thinking in terms of a brand launch—rather than a product launch—these pages offer a great recipe."

Michelle Wibel, CFSP, President, Nemco Food Equipment

A really great systematic approach to branding with a focus on food & beverage companies. The retail buyer quotes and perspectives add a very practical approach to the creating, producing, marketing and selling a product. Nice job!

Cary Gutwein, *President, Copper Moon Coffee*

"

In the local food-flooded market, voicing your own story is key to standing out in the sea of competing brands. But where do you begin? The first, and often hardest, step is articulating *why* you do what you do. No one can tell that story better than you, and this book will help. Nycz and his team at NewPoint are veterans at helping companies attain their foundational brand messaging. *Moving Your Brand Up the Food Chain* is an invaluable compass for orienting your brand and getting it on track."

Heather Tallman, *Indiana Grown Membership Development Program Manager, Indiana State Department of Agriculture*

It is as if a string of perfect miracles needs to happen for a successful new food product launch. Patrick's book is laid out in clear detail like a road map to achieve these goals.

Vince Ligas, *41 Years Retail Meat Industry*

As a former marketer at General Foods, as well as President of a Consumer Retail Package Company, I can tell you Patrick's book captures the essence of what regional food companies need to know to be successful marketing, selling and distributing their food products to retailers. This book could be re-titled, "Quick Review of Marketing Essentials for Successful Selling." Use this book as your constant reference during the entire life cycle of your food product line, and this will insure long term success.

Barrie Simpson, *Food & Consumer Products President, Retired*

Are you a small regional brand going up against the big guys? Want to expand your distribution and increase your margins? Read this book and learn how with Patrick and his NewPoint team helped double our retail sales 3 years in a row!

Randy Toleman, *Food Industry Consultant, Past V.P. Sales & Marketing, Mariah Packing Co & Indiana Packers Corp.*

Moving Your Brand Up the Food Chain™

© 2017 Patrick Nycz

All Rights Reserved.

No part of this publication may be reproduced, stored in a retrieval system, or transmitted, in any form or by any means, electronic, mechanical, photocopying, recording, or otherwise, without the written permission of the author.

First published by Dog Ear Publishing
4011 Vincennes Rd
Indianapolis, IN 46268
www.dogearpublishing.net

ISBN: 978-1-4575-5929-7

This book is printed on acid-free paper.

Printed in the United States of America

TABLE OF CONTENTS

Foreword ix
Preface xi

Section 1: Why Now for Local and Regional Food Brands
    Chapter 1:   Is This Book for You? 2
    Chapter 2:   Size and Location Matter 8
    Chapter 3:   The Buyer's Perspective 24
    Chapter 4:   Marketing Is Everything 37

Section 2: Brand Reconnaissance
    Chapter 5:   Internal Plans and Goals 48
    Chapter 6:   External Market Factors 59

Section 3: Brand Advantage Strategies
    Chapter 7:   Foundational Brand Development 72
    Chapter 8:   Branded Visual Identity 84
    Chapter 9:   Packaging 97
    Chapter 10:   Branded Campaigns 112

Section 4: Brand Growth Programs
    Chapter 11:   Brand Management 128
    Chapter 12:   Brand Activation 136
    Chapter 13:   Regional Brand Powerhouse 149
    Chapter 14:   Get Digital and Grow the Brand 155

Section 5: Brand Prosperity and Long-Term Growth
    Chapter 15:   Public Relations and Crisis Management 168
    Chapter 16:   Strategic Product Development 182

Acknowledgements 194
Index 195

FOREWORD

You're charged with profitably growing a developing food brand and you're not quite sure what to do next...

Relax! The next step is in your hands: Read this book.

Patrick Nycz has crafted this straightforward and easy to understand, practical guide to food brand marketing for food company owners, entrepreneurs, business managers, sales managers and yes, even food brand marketers. Patrick shares his knowledge and approach, honed from nearly 30 years of building consumer packaged brands and helping companies navigate the critical steps of consumer brand building.

In *Moving Your Brand Up the Food Chain*, you will discover why Patrick Nycz believes that the consumer and retail markets are ripe for developing and growing regional and local food brands. This book demonstrates how to capitalize on this trend with a strategic, consumer-based marketing foundation and approach. This book covers the waterfront of consumer brand marketing; it is both a road map and a quick reference guide discussing the critical topics along the path to developing a successful food brand.

Several times in my career, agencies have presented creative solutions and marketing tactics without doing the fundamental strategic work up front. As a result, they didn't truly understand who their client's target consumer actually was. Effective brand marketing just isn't developed that way. To build and grow profitable, vibrant and resilient food brands, it is imperative to choose a marketing partner who takes the right path. Patrick Nycz gets it and has practiced it throughout his professional marketing career.

If your current or a prospecting advertising agency is not proposing and following a brand development roadmap like the one Patrick Nycz lays out in his book, it's probably time for a change. They could actually be squandering your company's valuable financial resources by amplifying the wrong message or targeting the wrong consumers.

If your success and career depend on profitably growing and developing a food brand, *Moving Your Brand Up the Food Chain* by Patrick Nycz is a must-read.

Greg Metzger, August 2017

Greg Metzger is an accomplished brand marketing strategist and practitioner. Over a stellar career spanning more than 30 years, he has grown and expanded profitable regional brands in many highly competitive food categories including frozen food, spreads, salad dressing, beverage, snack foods, tomato products, condiments, sauces and salsa. He has held senior executive level marketing positions in several regionally and nationally recognized branded food companies. Greg is the former head of marketing for Indiana's own Red Gold Tomato Products Company. Based on his expertise, Greg has been quoted in the *Wall Street Journal.*

PREFACE

One of my fondest childhood memories is of my grandfather's A&P grocery store in Tiffin, Ohio. If we were lucky enough, my sister I would get to spend Saturday night at my grandparents' house, attend church the next morning, and then—the highlight of the day—we would stop by the store my grandfather managed. In the late 1960s, the store was always closed on Sundays. A closed grocery store is a magical place to a five- or six-year-old kid. We had the run of the place. Zipping up and down center-of-store aisles that were stacked tall with products, checking out our breath in the frozen food freezers and, of course, getting shooed away from the candy aisle and playing on the checkout lanes. I fell in love with the place.

Today, the grocery store aisle still has a hold on me. I can't just run in for a jar of spaghetti sauce or lettuce greens without pausing to check out a new product or packaging upgrade. If I am shopping for the week with my wife, she will hear me say "I'll catch up" more than once while I jot down a few notes in my phone or sneak a few pics of a new product. No other consumer retail outlet can match the supermarket as a highly competitive intersection of constantly evolving trends, innovation, and new product launches. The goal of this book is to help small, local, and emerging regional food brands grow market share within this consumer-driven space.

Maybe that's why I have spent my entire career working in the business of consumer-packaged goods (CPG) branding ranging from hardware, kitchen gadgets, office supplies to crafts, toys, games, and, of course, food. Whether working with established brands such as Ace Hardware, Master Lock, Rubbermaid, Wilson Sporting Goods, or

Hasbro, or with emerging brands in the food sector, one constant has remained clear:

The consumer may be king, but the retail and food service buyer is the gatekeeper. Therefore, it is in a supplier's best interest to know what a buyer cares about and is looking for in a supplier.

What exactly is a buyer looking for in a supplier? If you asked 10 manufacturing food salespeople this question, you would probably get 10 different answers. But if you asked 10 different food buyers the same question, you would probably only receive a few different answers. This book walks you through those buyers' answers as well as our third-party point of view on best practices for growing your brand.

In my experience acting as marketing and brand support for sales teams that sell into every type of retailer—small chains, mid-major regional stores, national big-box outlets—one constant stands out: buyers are looking for information in the form of category leadership, and category leadership only comes with doing your homework.

About homework, there comes a time when you'll realize that you must roll up your sleeves and do the real work to experience real success. This holds true even if it means stepping outside your comfort zone—and potentially on someone else's toes—to make an impact.

Homework started sooner than expected for me. Early in my career, the product team at Ace Hardware came back from a sourcing trip with 10 different bathroom hardware fixture sets: towel bars, toilet paper holders, and such all available in brass, stainless steel, and brushed nickel. Their job was to "pitch" the line to the stores. My firm was asked to create a branded program, name each line under the program, and develop the sell copy and packaging.

What does a young marketer with limited experience in bath hardware do in this situation? He dives in the trenches. In the days before the internet, it meant heading out to the hardware and department stores where these items were sold to learn as much as I could about the category. I learned about price points, product names, and packaging trends, and how the product was merchandised on the retail shelf as well as hitting the right perceived value with the packaging and branding.

With this type of homework ingrained in my work-DNA, I took a position at Warren Industries with its RoseArt-branded puzzle, craft, and game subsidiary. I started out as a creative director and oversaw the departments of research and development as well as creative services. I, then, became the director of marketing in the last half of my time with the organization. During my tenure at Warren, RoseArt became the No. 1 brand in the country with category management roles at Walmart and Meijer. However, we only got there by doing the work.

The leadership at Warren believed strongly in research across all areas of our category. That meant research into consumer attitudes and shopping habits, strategic planning that focused on our team's core competencies, as well as a pulse check of the category and competition through deep and thorough store checks. Although this information drove our product development and marketing, it was crucial that we packaged the information properly during our sales presentation meetings with buyers and positioned our team as experts in the category.

When Warren was bought by Mega Brands and it became apparent that our division was not a priority for the new leadership, I decided to utilize my knowledge and invest personally. I bought into an established marketing agency named Indiana Design Consortium (IDC Marketing for short) that placed a high value on collaborative data- and research-based return-on-investment (ROI) business growth strategies.

In business since 1972, IDC Marketing was first engaged by its clients to identify unmet or underserved needs for food-service supplies and equipment, and then to design product solutions that meet those needs. The resulting products included many innovations in food safety and food-service employee safety, such as the blue Wear-Ever® Cool Handle (licensed for manufacture by Lincoln Foodservice Products, Inc.).

IDC Marketing has worked in multiple categories and industries throughout the years, but it has always maintained a roster of food manufacturers/processors and food-service equipment manufacturers as its solid client base. Our marketing firm's motto is "Strategy First", which means the company philosophy leans heavily on becoming an expert in our client's category and then aligning their brand for success.

New Focus, New Direction: NewPoint

More than 45 years of proven success with our food industry client partners, coupled with data showing significant growth in the food production and distribution sector particularly for local, regional brands, has inspired my team to form a new company called NewPoint. The competitive and always evolving food industry is its sole focus.

NewPoint is a collection of seasoned strategists and creatives who have one goal—to Move Your Brand Up the Food Chain™. NewPoint is a full-service strategic marketing and branding firm with deep focus and concentration on the food industry sector. The core values of IDC Marketing remain: NewPoint is in the business of growing your business.

Section 1

Why Now for Local and Regional Food Brands

Chapter 1

IS THIS BOOK FOR YOU?

Is this book for you? It could be if you answer yes to the following questions:

- Do you sell a food product to retailers and/or food service outlets?
- Do you ever wonder why the buyer, or gatekeeper, passes on your product and opts for the product offered by your competitors instead?
- Are you interested in hearing what grocery merchandising and food service procurement professionals are looking for and possibly missing from their food supplier partners?

This book could also be for you if you answer no to these questions:

- Are you at your top capacity in terms of food shipments?
- Does your brand/label own or share the top market share in your local market's grocery aisle?
- Do you know why your top customers, including your end-line consumers, prefer your product over the product offered by your competitors?
- Are you procuring top pricing?
- Do you understand how to leverage macro and consumer food trends into sales for your product?

I tackle these questions within the chapters of this book. And, although I have been on the front lines as a director of marketing for many consumer products, this book is not simply filled with personal anecdotes about the tricks and tips used to support the sale of a product. Such information will not help you because your products, region, customers, and internal sales, operations, and distribution models are all different from those I've worked with in the past.

I took the same approach to this book that NewPoint takes to the work we do with our client partners—I did the homework. I talked to grocery merchandising and food service procurement professionals. I asked them the following questions:

- What is the buyer looking for in a branded food partner?
- What are pros and cons to being a local or regional food brand supplier?
- What are two or three questions you wish food manufacturers (current or new) would ask?

Although I asked these questions while composing this book, I also intend to keep asking questions on a regular basis—probably every six months or so—because the food industry is not a static environment. It is fluid.

At NewPoint, we've found that whenever we ask grocery merchandising and food service procurement professionals these questions, their answers change. Sometimes their answers are based on the buyer's corporate goals for the current cycle. Their answers are also influenced by a myriad of other things such as the general competitive supermarket landscape, consumer trends, company initiatives on evolving government regulations for labeling and food safety, as well as local sourcing, transparency, and so on.

Ultimately, this book is for you if you want to move your brand up the food chain. It's for when you ask the biggest question of all: is now the time to accelerate growth? Only you and your team will know.

The indicators are there. Product sales are growing steadily. Customers are asking for more from your company. Your business has started to bump up against the big chains more often. It's not unusual for a smaller, local or a regional player to be viewed as a commodity or a "value" brand. Are you happy with that designation?

Most of the companies NewPoint works with have higher aspirations. They want to mean something more to their customers. They are focused on customer service. They strive to partner with the gatekeepers in the food industry and provide good products at a fair price.

Often, however, these companies encounter a capacity issue and not the type involving the company's operations. These companies do not have a processing, manufacturing, or a sales issue. They simply do not have the capacity to create a sustainable and engaging marketing strategy. Most of these executive teams running regional food companies have excellent leadership, great operations teams, and awesome sales teams. They truly believe that they have better and/or different products and that they just need help in marketing, which can make the difference between being a selling business that grows and one that remains a small commodity product line. Unfortunately, these executives simply don't know what to say when the gatekeepers—the grocery merchandising and food service procurement professionals—ask them why it should be their product, and not the competitor's product, on the shelf.

In the highly competitive world of the food industry, brand equals margin, and marketing makes the brand.

You should continue reading if you want to learn how to make informed decisions in areas such as positioning your company against competitors, product packaging, and leveraging macro and consumer food trends. These are all aspects of marketing strategies that will help transform your product line into a brand and create a demonstrable difference in how your line is viewed by the buyer. When this happens, it can signal that your company's product line is emerging as a true brand, which, in turn, can signify the upward price flexibility and margins associated with being a name-brand product.

Within this book, I address numerous topics aimed at helping local, smaller, and regional food brands propel themselves up the food chain. The topics have been divided into general sections, including an industry overview, brand reconnaissance, brand advantage strategies, brand growth programs, and brand prosperity and long-term planning. We will proceed as follows:

Chapter 2: Size and Location Matter. In the past five years, smaller brands and private brand manufacturers grew more rapidly than the 25 biggest U.S. food and beverage manufacturers. This translates to the top 25 food brand manufacturers losing a 3.5 percent market share to their smaller competitors. The opportunity for growth is there.

Chapter 3: The Buyer's Perspective. Here I analyze the interviews NewPoint conducted with retail buyers, distributors, and brokers. I also discuss what differentiates manufacturers and how a company leverages that differentiation.

Chapter 4: Marketing Is Everything. How can a small brand compete with the big-budget well-known brands? By taking a page from their marketing book and developing a strong brand through an effective strategic marketing plan. Marketing isn't the only way to elevate a brand, but it can mean everything.

Chapter 5: Internal Plans and Goals. Big picture—where do you want to be? Is your goal a larger market share or increased profits? You must know what goals are to create your internal plan. Then you can decide what the internal challenges you'll need to face to reach your goal.

Chapter 6: External Market Factors. What are your external market factors? Learn how to establish product differentiation through industry, category, competitive and trend analysis.

Chapter 7: Foundational Brand Development. Ascertain your true and clear brand strength, brand position, brand promise, and brand message. Using these discoveries, you can develop a brand that resonates with your core target audience and differentiates you from the competition.

Chapter 8: Branded Visual Identity. Consistency in your brand's visual identity is vital to developing and nurturing a loyal consumer base. Develop your logo, packaging, sales support materials, and other aspects of a visual brand identity by establishing consistent styles, fonts, colors, and visual imagery for your product.

Chapter 9: Packaging. Learn how to stand out and make a lasting impression in just a few seconds, while also understanding the importance of product labeling and food safety.

Chapter 10: Branded Campaigns. Creating marketing messages emphasizes your brand's essence and appeal to its core audience. Here, I'll discuss the importance of both digital and traditional marketing channels, and familiarize you with the Brand Affinity Matrix.

Chapter 11: Brand Management. In this chapter, you'll discover the role that brand managers play, including their responsibilities, keys to their success, and common brand management mistakes. Effective brand management can turn a manufacturer that simply makes something into one that *is* something.

Chapter 12: Brand Activation. To aid in your brand's growth, you need to build a complete brand marketing plan and support sales. Here, I'll cover developing a plan that addresses activation strategies, awareness tactics, engagement, couponing, buyer presentations, and other tactics to package your brand's campaign.

Chapter 13: Regional Brand Powerhouse. Learn to dominate your chosen region by defining your target area and concentrating on it through focused marketing and grassroots tactics. Then you create your plan for sales, marketing, and operations growth.

Chapter 14: Get Digital and Grow the Brand. To further add growth through advertising, embrace digital marketing by developing social media and other online engagement strategies. You can create a circle of consumer feedback and response, cultivate brand evangelists, and improve your customer service all through social media.

Chapter 15: Public Relations and Crisis Management. In this chapter, I discuss a content strategy for customer and consumer communications, ranging from promotions and new product on the shelves to consumer complaints and recalls.

Chapter 16: Strategic Product Development. Growth happens through innovation. In this chapter, I'll teach you to develop new products by identifying your ideal customer, tracking and leveraging trends, discussing your buyer's needs and preferences, and engaging in effective and efficient development.

Chapter 2

SIZE AND LOCATION MATTER

> *"It's harder to compete with the big guys when you are a smaller supplier. It's harder to expand into other markets, where consumers may not be familiar with your name versus a national brand. But a lot of the national (retailers) today want what's regional. So it can be done. Absolutely."*
>
> —M. M., senior buyer, 22 years' experience

It began with your vision—a food enthusiast's dream of launching a product line. Combined with your entrepreneurial spirit and a lot of hard work, you have transformed that vision into reality. Your original vision is now a branded product line that landed on store shelves and is rubbing elbows with the food industry's heavy hitters.

However, that once-satisfying elbow rubbing has developed into more of a jostling for space as the vision for your brand collides with the seemingly unstoppable forces of national food producers. Getting to where you are now was hard enough. Why should you think that battling with the heavy hitters is even possible?

Here's why: There has never been a better time to do so. Currently, an almost overwhelming number of market indicators suggest that there's an unprecedented amount of volatility in the industry. This shift is consumer-driven, and it has caused everything to evolve:

- A 2015 U.S. Census Bureau report stated that millennials, the demographic of young people born in between 1985 and 2000 with the highest familiarity of emerging technologies in digital, mobile and social media, already outnumbered baby boomers by nearly 10 million, so consumer demographics are definitely changing.

- Driven in part by the rise of millennials, consumer tastes and preferences are varying. Consumers are showing an increased desire for local products made by companies that are transparent, socially relevant, and flexible.
- Avenues for marketing and advertising are developing, with the relatively inexpensive avenues within digital media becoming increasingly relevant.
- Opinions and attitudes toward traditional national food companies are evolving, with consumers showing high levels of distrust in those companies and their brands.
- These evolving factors—the increasing influence of millennials, the desire for local products, the rise of digital media, and a distrust in "Big Food"—add up to significant leverage for local, small, local or regional companies like yours. For you, change is good.

By "Big Food" I'm referencing the national, entrenched brands we've seen on the shelves for decades. And Big Food does not like change. Think of them as the ocean liners of the food product industry, where everything is done on a massive scale and tradition reigns. The problem with ocean liners is that once moving they are very set in their ways. They are slow to adjust when the weather shifts and sailing is no longer smooth. Well, the weather has most certainly shifted, and the national brand ocean liners are now more vulnerable than ever.

Now is the time to strike. Many industry analysts say that today's volatility does more than just create an opportunity for you and your brand. They believe it's a near-necessity that you act upon that volatility, with some of them comparing the current rise of smaller food brands to the high-tech start-up boom in Silicon Valley not so long ago.

The reasons why you and your brand should make the leap and take on the heavy hitters are both numerous and varied. They touch on every aspect of the ever-evolving food industry, from initial production to final purchase. In this chapter, we will explore these reasons in detail.

THE NUMBERS

While I will talk at length in this chapter about sociological trends and professional opinions, it's basic mathematics that can provide the most convincing argument that now is the time to bolster your brand. The numbers themselves may seem small—a few percentage points here and there. Yet, these points add up to tens of millions of dollars that small and mid-sized regional food companies are already siphoning off from their larger national competitors, and big business is beginning to take notice.

Using various analysis techniques and applying them to different aspects of the food industry at different times, several top research institutions and other interested parties have arrived at the following findings:

U.S. Department of Agriculture (USDA)

According to industry analyst Food Dive, the USDA predicts that the sales of locally produced foods, which hit $12 billion in 2014, will surge to $20 billion by 2019.

Deloitte Consulting, Food Marketing Institute, and the Grocery Manufacturers Association

An exhaustive industry study was conducted in 2015, focusing on evolving consumer trends. During their study, Deloitte found that smaller and private food brand manufacturers grew more rapidly (4.0 percent growth), than the 25 biggest U.S. food and beverage manufacturers (1.0 percent growth) between 2009 and 2013.

A.T. Kearney and The Hartman Group

A.T. Kearney and The Hartman Group found that medium and small companies grew at a faster rate than the top 25 U.S. food manufacturers between 2012 and 2015. The Hartman Group found that medium and small companies grew 11 to 15 percent more compared to just 1.8 percent growth for the larger ones. In terms of total revenue growth, the amount for medium and small companies ($14 billion) almost equaled that of the top manufacturers ($16 billion).

Financial Times

According to *Financial Times*, the Boston Consulting Group released research reporting that between 2011 and 2015, $18 billion in sales shifted from large packaged goods companies to smaller businesses. That number amounts to a 2.7 percentage-point loss for the big companies.

Jeffries

According to a 2015 *New York Times* piece, the global investment bank Jeffries reported that the big brands lost their market share to new products in 42 of 54 categories over the previous five years.

Rabobank

International industry analyst Rabobank reported that, according to the market intelligence, data and analytics firm Information Resources, Inc. (IRI), the market share increase for small and mid-sized companies in 2014 amounted to a $5 billion increase in sales.

Food Processing

Among the largest publicly traded companies on *Food Processing* magazine's top 100 list, no fewer than one-third reported sales declines in 2014, while most of the others registered only modest gains. Among those suffering declines were top-50 companies such as Kraft foods (No. 8), General Mills (No. 10), Kellogg's (No. 13), and Heinz (No. 27). Aggregate sales declines totaled more than $1.7 billion, a 2.2 percent drop from 2013.

In the same study, *Food Processing* stated that Dow Jones VentureSource reported venture capital investments in small food companies totaling nearly $377 million in 2014. That total had more than doubled since 2013, and VentureSource projected another doubling of the investment in 2015.

BEYOND THE NUMBERS

What has driven the money train's change in direction? Consumer tastes and preferences. In their respective studies, Deloitte, A.T. Kearney and the Hartman Group, and Rabobank all addressed the potential implications of the shift in consumer preferences. Deloitte predicted that the marketplace would continue to fragment along the lines of evolving factors. A.T. Kearney and the Hartman Group accentuated the increasing preference for local products. Citing the rise of millennials and the reluctance of big companies to adapt, Rabobank viewed the future of these companies as increasingly troubled. In general, the analysts arrived at the same conclusion: smaller, regional, and local food companies like yours are an increasingly influential force within the marketplace.

Deloitte

According to the Deloitte study, the days of dominance for the traditional value drivers among consumers—price, taste and convenience—are numbered. Instead, the evolving value drivers of health and wellness, food safety, social impact, experience, and transparency are increasingly important. Roughly 50 percent of consumers now weigh these evolving drivers, which were once considered a niche portion of the market, more heavily than the traditional ones.

Furthermore, while Deloitte's report stated that the shift toward the evolving drivers took place over all age groups and geographic areas, that percentage is bound to increase as millennials become a larger portion of the consuming public. The Deloitte study suggests that they are partial to the evolving drivers. Millennials, by the way, already outnumber baby boomers within the U.S. population. According to Deloitte, the potential implications of its findings include the following:

* Consumer tastes and preferences will continue to fragment along the lines of evolving value drivers.
* Consumers who place more value on evolving drivers appear more likely to use social media, mobile applications, and digital sources to acquire information on the path to purchase.
* Consumers who place more value on evolving drivers are more prone to distrust the food industry in general.
* Market success will be determined by building purpose-driven competitive advantages.

Smaller newer companies will leverage new technologies, third-party relationships, and improved engagement to earn customer trust and compete in the market.

A.T. Kearney and The Hartman Group

A.T. Kearney recently conducted a pair of studies that focused on local products and smaller food production companies. The first, which was conducted in 2015, was titled "Firmly Rooted, the Local Food Market Expands". The second, "Is Big Food in Trouble?", was conducted jointly with The Hartman Group in 2016. Together, the studies reported good news for smaller companies like yours. According to the 2015 study ...

*Almost all consumers (93 percent) associate local with fresh, and fresh is the No. 1 purchasing factor for grocery consumers by far.

*Approximately 78 percent of shoppers are willing to pay more for local food.

*Being local is an increasingly important attribute for not just produce, meat, and seafood, but also prepared foods and dry goods. According to the 2016 study conducted with The Hartman Group:

- * More foods are being launched that go beyond basic nutrition, increasingly following dynamic trends and consumer preferences.
- * Locally sourced foods with a direct-to-consumer model are becoming more attractive.
- * The demand for transparency in food sourcing, production, and labeling is gaining traction.
- * Consumers are discovering novel and foreign ingredients at an increasing rate.

The Hartman Group/Food Marketing Institute

The Hartman Group also partnered with the Food Marketing Institute on a 2017 study of trends in U.S. grocery shopper behavior as they apply to the various aspects of supplier transparency. While the study saw a general desire among shoppers for increased transparency in general, the two companies also came to the following conclusions.

Consumers were most concerned with those aspects of transparency that were related to what's within products, as opposed to those aspects that were related to the societal practices of a company that produced it. Products free of contaminants and those that met a family's dietary needs were also primary factors.

For more than 67 percent of shoppers, buying local products relates to their desire for a greater understanding about a connection to their food. Shoppers like knowing where their food comes from, how it is grown, and how it is produced. Buying local is believed to support local economies and build the vitality of local communities.

Shoppers tend to perceive local food producers as being smaller in scale than large national companies, and therefore are viewed as being more personally passionate, accountable, and committed to quality.

Rabobank

The 2015 Rabobank study, titled "Dude, Where's My Consumer? Remaining Relevant to Today's U.S. Consumer", is perhaps the most critical among these studies when it comes to exposing the weaknesses of large food manufacturers. It's particularly interesting because, like the A.T. Kearney reports, it was conducted with the future health of the heavy hitters themselves in mind. Rabobank's study, which opened with the sentence "Many of America's largest food and beverage companies are in trouble," included the following findings.

One of the most important changes in the market is the rise in purchasing power of the 75-million strong millennial generation. Millennials are more experimental in their choices, more health conscious, and appear to be willing to spend a greater share of their income on food.

Social media is the principal source driving the acceleration in consumer trends, and digital conversation between friends, family, and followers through social media is fast becoming every brand's most cost-effective marketing arena and source of criticism.

The growing number of alternative distribution and retail options has created new opportunities for emerging brands, giving these products the chance to grow rapidly as mainstream national retailers (Walmart, Kroger, Costco, etc.) use them to differentiate themselves.

Smaller companies have proven adept at spotting and responding to new trends and gaps in the market. Large companies may still be too wedded to their iconic brands and entrenched in their traditional ways, leaving them slow to react to the evolving marketplace.

Consumer attitudes towards food companies have evolved, with consumers, millennials in particular, showing an increasing preference for small specialized operators that passionately sell their mission to provide better-quality and ethical products.

TREND ANALYSIS

In today's world of limitless information and hyper-speed communication, specific food trends are shifting as rapidly as ever. However, there are several general trends in consumer tastes and preferences that have opened the door for smaller and more local manufacturers. They are a preference for locally produced items; an affinity for fresh, natural, and healthy alternatives; and a desire for increased transparency on the part of the manufacturer.

The overwhelming consumer preference for local products has been highlighted by the numbers and analysis stated previously. Additionally, a 2015 USDA survey that weighed heavily on a 2011 report by the Food Marketing Institute found that over 80 percent of grocery store shoppers reported purchasing local foods occasionally while 9 percent bought local foods whenever possible. Eight-three percent of shoppers cited freshness as the most frequent reason for their preference for local goods. Local means fresh to consumers, and fresh is by far their top purchasing factor followed by supporting local businesses. Retailers also consider freshness important, not only because the consumer does, but because it simplifies their purchasing process. Furthermore, by nature the terms *local* and *fresh* also suggests healthier and less-processed food. In short, local is a built-in position from which to launch your brand.

Similarly, just as the term *local* is closely associated with fresh in the eyes of consumers, so is transparency associated with trust and authenticity. Analysis has shown that today's consumers are increasingly distrustful of large companies, instead favoring small companies that have authenticity and a social conscience built into their mission. According to a 2015 piece in *Advertising Age* magazine, the industry analysis company Sanford C. Bernstein concluded that the tipping point for consumer trust in Big Food dated back to 2013. It was then, the analyst claims, that the shift away from heavily processed foods, which to many consumers means Big Food, became more evident. Consumers were more educated and better connected, and they were no longer willing to settle for what they saw as the status quo. By building on the trust of your existing consumer base and practicing continued transparency, you can use this as another launch platform and fill that trust gap.

The 2017 study by The Hartman Group and the Food Marketing Institute previously mentioned further reinforces the rising value of transparency. The fact that shoppers tend to perceive local food producers as being smaller in scale than large national companies; and therefore, as being more personally passionate, accountable, and committed to quality; is arguably the study's most crucial finding. This perception is important because perception is reality in our world, insofar as what you are selling to consumers is both a product and the idea of that product. If shoppers tend to think local companies are more passionate, accountable, and committed to quality, then a smaller company like yours can build on and leverage this existing perception. I will address ways to do this, as well as transparency, in more detail later in this book.

Even when it comes to those more specific and elusive trends, smaller manufacturers seem to have an advantage over their larger competitors because their smaller size often makes them more flexible and quicker to react. Whereas a larger company might be reluctant to adopt new ideas and then need time to adapt when it does, smaller companies are often more willing to embrace change and are nimble enough to act fast.

Marketing Trends

Analysis has also suggested that trends in marketing practices have changed in a way that favors smaller and local manufacturers. Traditional advertising is becoming increasingly irrelevant to consumers, particularly millennials. At the same time, social media is gaining in relevance as a marketing method, a fact that large companies have often failed to use to their advantage. Social media marketing programs are vital, and they are built into the marketing plans of many smaller companies as they move away from traditional and more expensive marketing methods. Social media is also something that, like the growth of many a small company, is grassroots in nature because it begins at the peer level. I will discuss marketing strategies in general, and grassroots tactics later in this book.

Your Retailers

Just like the industry analysts, many of the retailers you'll work with have recognized the market trends and see the benefits offered by smaller companies like yours. In general, the retailers NewPoint talked to appreciate the flexibility of production and the willingness to develop new products that smaller companies like yours should offer.

While there are obvious advantages to the overall volume and consistency they enjoy when dealing with larger manufacturers, the retailers we talked to also saw the benefits of dealing with smaller companies because they are more flexible. Product freshness, variable batch size, and fluctuating consumer demand, retailers said, are all factors that smaller companies often handle better than their plodding national competitors.

Our retailers also favored smaller manufactures over large ones when it came to innovative product development and the ability to capitalize on trends in consumer preferences. As we have shown, larger more well-established companies are naturally hesitant to tweak a product line that has proven successful in the past. Smaller manufacturers, the retailers believe, are more willing to change and innovate as they attempt to fulfill their entrepreneurial vision.

IN THEIR OWN WORDS: Retailers on the advantages of local and regional manufacturers

> *"On the pro side, (local and regional brand manufacturers) are more in tune with the local businesses and consumers. In a lot of cases, they have a shorter lead time, which is also quicker to the shelf. In almost all cases, they are able to produce in smaller batch sizes, which entails that it gives you fresher product."*
>
> C. S., buyer, 18 years' experience

> "If ... the buy-local trend is what's driving the higher percentage numbers, then that would mean that you should be paying more attention to the local guys that are coming in and knocking on your door. You need to see what the opportunities are because, if people are getting that feel-good attitude from buying the local applesauce or whatever it might be, then you need to make sure you have that for them. If the numbers are growing that way, then it makes perfect sense."
>
> **B. D., senior buyer, 23 years' experience**

> "It's definitely a necessity to look at smaller regional brands, for many reasons. Because it hits home or they can hit a lot of criteria. Maybe they are offering an organic or a product that some of the big guys aren't thinking about. The big guys might just go after that great big carrot, and the smaller guys are going to fit the niches of the retailers."
>
> **S. T., buyer, 17 years' experience**

SUCCESS STORIES

It's popular in food industry circles to rave about Chobani yogurt's rise from zero sales to sales of more than $5 billion in less than five years as the benchmark. For every Chobani, however, there are scores of other upstart brands that started small but possess similarly grand visions. What follows are just a few prime examples of how local, smaller, and regional companies can build their brand in today's dynamic marketplace.

Nellino's Sauce Co.

Neal McTighe of Raleigh, North Carolina, turned a love of all things Italian into Nello's Sauce Co., a tiny pasta sauce company, in 2010. According to a 2015 *New York Times* article focused on the emergence of small food companies, McTighe left his job in publishing to develop a red sauce based on a family recipe and started selling the homemade sauce online. He sold $750 of Nello's Sauce in the first month.

Four years later when he tired of producing the sauces by himself, McTighe hired a small contract manufacturing company that was willing to produce in small batches. After receiving original investments from family and friends, Whole Foods eventually gave McTighe and his company a $30,000 loan to support the development of an heirloom tomato sauce. With the preservation of product quality in mind rather than demand, Nello's Sauce planned a limited run of 20,000 to 25,000 jars per release in 2015.

According to its website, McTighe changed the name of his company to Nellino's Sauce Co. and unveiled a new packaging scheme for its vegan, organic, and gluten-free sauce line in 2017. Nellino's website states that the company grew from being available online only to being available at local and then regional retail outlets. After partnering with national retail powerhouses such as Costco and Kroger among others, Nellino's now claims to be a top national premium sauce company.

Cherryvale Farms

Cherryvale Farms is a locally grown Santa Cruz, California-based baking mix company that was started in 2010 by former public relations processional Lindsey Rosenberg. According to the 2015 *New York Times* piece mentioned previously, the company's original production process included one Hobart mixer, a commercial kitchen space Rosenberg rented for four overnight hours daily, and her own kitchen table. Rosenberg's mother served as her assistant, and her husband, a marketing consultant, designed the packaging.

The first retailer to pick up Rosenberg's mixes, which began as all-organic and later went vegan, was a small natural foods grocery chain. Cherryvale Farms then moved into 70 Whole Foods stores. Eventually,

Rosenberg began creating her mixes full-time in a commercial kitchen and packaging them in a warehouse, and Cherryvale Farms began appearing in more than 1,200 stores nationwide by 2015. According to a 2016 blog on its website, Cherryvale Farms partnered with nearly 2,000 stores in 2016.

Downeast Cider House

Downeast Cider House is a Boston-based hard cider company that started as a dorm-room hobby for three millennial college students in 2011 and quickly swept through its region. According to simultaneous articles in the *Boston Globe* and *Boston* Magazine, the trio avoided what they called "real jobs" and opted instead to launch their own brand. Their goals were to take advantage of what they saw as a lack of brand loyalty in the burgeoning hard-cider market and to produce pure fresh-pressed and all-natural cider.

Operating out of a small Maine power mill with the three millennials as the only employees, Downeast began with a single-cider line that was originally sold store-to-store in the Boston area. The company has grown every year since its inception, averaging 75 percent growth between 2011 and 2016, and has already had to move its operations three times to increasingly larger facilities to meet capacity. Downeast, which now has approximately 200 full- and part-time employees, currently operates out of a 16,500-square foot Boston plant that produces 350,000 cases of cider in several varieties per year.

Not surprisingly, Downeast landed at No. 6 on the Inc.com list of the 10 fastest growing companies in the food and beverage industry for 2016. The growing company, whose cider is already available throughout New England, plans on expanding to New York, Chicago, Texas, Colorado, and California, with the hopes of eventually selling more than one million cases per year.

CONCLUSION

Whether you are a small food company looking to grow its brand or simply an entrepreneur with a vision, there has never been a better time than right now to act. The number crunchers and analysts are all saying that consumer preferences are changing in your favor. The industry bigwigs have realized it, and they are worrying. Investors have realized it, and they are spending. Your retailers have realized it, and they are buying. Why should you think that doing battle with the heavy hitters is even possible? Because it absolutely is.

Chapter 3

THE BUYER'S PERSPECTIVE

Your buyers and retailers are arguably the most important people you will deal with as you make your move up the food chain. They are the gatekeepers that stand between your products and the end-line consumer, and the growth of your company and its branded products depends on the success you have working with them. Before you can sell to your consumers, you must first sell to them.

There is good news and bad news when it comes to selling to your buyers/retailers. The good news is that your buyers and retailers are just as interested as you are in taking advantage of the rising influence of local, smaller, and regional companies. The bad news is that they must be convinced that your products are more promising than those offered by your many competitors. In my experience, the best way to sell to buyers and retailers is to understand the needs and desires motivating them. To that end, I asked numerous buyers and retailers, as well as some brokers and distributors, a battery of questions designed to reveal the driving factors when they are deciding which companies to partner with.

What follows is an excerpt from the list of questions I asked, along with some interpretation and analysis of their answers.

Question 1: What sources do you use for industry news and category information (websites, magazines, reports, etc.)?

It probably goes without saying, but it pays to be dialed into the same information sources as the people to which you're selling. That said, subscribing to your category trade magazine is the most important source you can look at because you can bet that all the buyers are doing this as well. Industry news and trends are vital pieces of information in making decisions about what goes on the shelf, and trend magazines are the best place to source it. *Supermarket News* and *Progressive Grocer* also provide a lot of category and trend information. In addition, Nielsen, IRI, and Food Market Institute (FMI) are also primary sources for general information and industry-wide analysis. Many of the buyers and retailers we spoke with still depend on these traditional sources for their information, using online and other digital research only as needed.

Question 2: What decisions or factors determine your need for a new supplier?

Simply put, it behooves you to be well-positioned with a buyer when they are getting ready to make a switch. You may not know when that time will come, but it helps to be on the buyer's shortlist of potential replacements. Some of the reasons our buyers and retailers cited for replacing a supplier included consumer complaints, poor sales, and a lack of flexibility in order fulfillment and restocking. From a marketing viewpoint, our suggestion would be to build your presentations by addressing how your company is willing to work with its buyers and retailers when such issues arise.

Question 3: What qualifications does it take to become a new supplier (outside of typical supplier qualifications)?

Judging from the widely varied reactions we received from this question, this should be one of the first questions you ask yourself and your buyers and retailers. Some qualifications that were mentioned revolved around proper certifications, operations capacity, and a supplier's ability and willingness to provide private label products. There were also many other responses, but the ultimate point is that each buyer/retailer has their own unique set of qualifications, which is why this question is such an important one to ask. It's been an important question to ask when I've been able to present to everyone from a small independent chain to a Walmart or Kroger. Even new buyers working for a longtime partner company are going to have new metrics for the qualifications they are seeking in partners.

Question 4: What defines a good supplier?

Many of the answers we received during our survey with buyers and retailers suggest good business practices go a long way toward a good business relationship. While building a personal relationship with the buyer is important, proving that you are an expert in your category is vital, while being first-to-market or otherwise innovative is a plus. Also, developing presentations and driving the conversation towards turns on shelves and putting their business first, as well as thinking about mutually beneficial opportunities and future planning to grow business together, should be top priorities.

Question 5: What are two to three questions you wish current or new food manufacturers would ask?

This was kind of a hot-button question, and NewPoint received a variety of good answers. "How can we partner for future growth?" and "What product innovations are you looking for?" were two of the more common questions our buyers and retailers wished suppliers would ask. Basically, it all seems to boil down to this question: "What do you need?" Buyer and retailers want you to put their interests first and understand their highly competitive retail business. They want you to treat them with respect by not simply waltzing into a meeting and expecting your product to be put on shelf, and they don't want to feel like you've wasted their time.

Question 6: What are two to three things you wish food manufacturers knew about your job?

One commonality stood out here: buyers and retailers are busy people. Many of the buyers and retailers we spoke to mentioned how limited their time and resources are. Thus, having a basic understanding of their limited time and showing respect is imperative to developing a good business relationship. Your primary concern may be getting your product listed in their retail product roster, also known as their planogram. However, the buyer across the table from you is pressed for time and feeling corporate pressure to be competitive in the increasingly margin-starved grocery industry. As we will see in upcoming questions, a smaller food manufacturer or supplier can use this fact to differentiate itself from the big guys.

Question 7: How much of the responsibility of moving their product off the shelf, into the cart, and ultimately through the checkout is on food manufacturers to support retails sales? What support methods do you prefer?

This question came directly from a conversation I had with a buyer several years ago. He told me point-blank that it was my job, and not his job, to move products off the shelf, into the cart, and through the checkout. This buyer expressed frustration at what he perceived as a long line of supplier partners whose only concern seemed to be getting the product into his planogram.

The responses I received from the buyers and retailers I interviewed for this book were not nearly so extreme. At most, buyers thought the job was a 50:50 proposition. However, buyers clearly believe that manufacturers and suppliers should take some ownership over end-line sales. This sentiment stems from the spirit of partnership that many buyers and retailers are looking for. Since small companies like yours ought to be thinking about building their power base and expanding product offerings with key retail partners anyway, it makes sense that they take some ownership as a way of showing support for their partners.

Question 8: How much does consumer marketing by a food manufacturer affect your decision to list their product?

This may seem like a no-brainer question. First, a marketing guy is asking it. Second, what buyers are going to respond "none needed" to this question? Yet, the reality is that there must be a balance. If marketing adds too much to the cost, then the buyer is not going be able to justify adding your product their planogram. Then again, buyers and retailers want to see that you are committed to the success of your products. A local manufacturer can make a big impact by starting small with a regional marketing plan. Marketing costs should be proportional to product cost and retail pricing, and marketing plans should be flexible enough to allow for amplification or shrinkage as the situation warrants.

Question 9: How much does a food manufacturer conducting consumer research affect your decision to list their products?

I don't think anyone's ever had a negative answer to this question. Consumer research is a huge part of being an expert in your category, and buyers and retailers love experts. Big Food companies have consumer research built into their marketing and product development budgets. Smaller companies can certainly counter that at a lower cost by leveraging existing data from IRI, FMI, Nielsen, and trade publications. Additionally, there are numerous grassroots or otherwise inexpensive marketing research techniques that can be utilized to connect directly with consumers. Visit retail stores and do store checks. Survey your loyalty club, talk directly to your biggest fans on Facebook, or arrange a store intercept with your small independent retail partners.

Question 10: How much of the job requires food manufacturers to be experts in their category, and how do the best manufacturers show their expertise?

Buyer answers to the first question were unanimous and absolute: 100 percent of the responsibility is on the food manufacturers to be experts in their category. The fact is, the more you are an expert in your category—from the target market, the planogram, the competition, and trends to your product's differentiation and packaging—the more you position yourself and your company as an excellent resource to the buyer. Gaining expertise and leveraging it are among the key concepts driving this book, and buyers and retailers believe that there's no reason to even be in business with them if you aren't an expert. Buyers don't want to educate you on your category, which might sound like an obvious requirement. However, several buyers told me it was laughable how many suppliers simply don't know their own business—an issue that seems to happen more often as supplier sales teams change and become more inexperienced with each passing year.

As far as showing expertise, a good game plan is to package your buyer presentations so that they accentuate your category expertise. This means you must prove to them that you have a firm grasp on all the data, trend information, and consumer feedback mentioned in Question 9. In short, be prepared to back up your product presentation with a convincing argument.

Question 11: What are the pros and cons to being a national food brand supplier?

In many ways, the buyers and retailers I interviewed spoke from both sides of their mouths when it came to the attributes of national suppliers. They generally liked the fact that national suppliers had bigger budgets, could produce a variety of related products in bulk, and came with built-in brand recognition. However, many buyers and retailers also said that the drawbacks, which came with national suppliers, included inefficient spending, demand-side product shortages, a potential lack of product freshness, and the fact that their products are available everywhere.

Our advice to local or regional manufacturers would be to leverage the cons of national suppliers and counter the pros by presenting a comprehensive plan for increasing your brand's recognition and voicing your willingness to broaden your product line (if possible).

Question 12: What are the pros and cons to being a local or regional food brand supplier?

This question ties directly to Question 11. The most obvious factor here, according to our buyers and retailers, came down to brand recognition. Most them believed that strong local and regional brand recognition was a major asset for smaller manufacturers, while also claiming that weak national brand recognition was a major drawback. Many liked the fact that smaller manufacturers could offer unique and often fresher products, while also showing a greater willingness to innovate and align with industry trends. Many also worried about the limited operations capacity and ability to grow that they believe comes with smaller companies.

My advice here is much like my advice for Question 11: expose the cons of the national suppliers and leverage the pros of smaller companies like yours. Counter buyer and retailer doubts about brand recognition and operations capacity by showing them plans for growth, which I will discuss later in-depth. Both questions about buyer/retailer perceptions of national versus regional food brand suppliers should be part of the communication you have with them. Such communication is the foundation of strong manufacturer and gatekeeper partnerships.

Question 13: How important is size, capacity, and location of a supplier? What are some of the factors that would eliminate a supplier from meeting your qualifications?

I addressed this briefly during earlier analysis. If a small food company is going to muscle its way into a retail planogram, it's going to have to deal with one potentially damaging perception held by many buyers: the perception that small companies struggle when it comes to size, capacity, and location. Buyers should consider whether a smaller manufacturer can successfully grow as a company, and if that company has the operations capacity to meet their growth goals. Buyers also must think about the distance between a manufacturer's facility and their nearest retail outlet or storage site. Distance can impact timeliness, freshness, and overall costs.

My advice to you is to address this perception in your buyer presentations and discuss it during meetings so that you can alter that perception and build trust. Having a plan for growth goes a long way toward showing that you have these areas secure.

Question 14: What do you think of this fact?

Smaller brand manufacturers grew more rapidly at 4.9 percent than the 25 biggest U.S. food and beverage manufacturers who averaged only 1 percent annual growth from 2009 to 2013. This translates to the top 25 food brand manufacturers losing 3.5% market share.

This little nugget of truth represents the backbone of my argument within this book, as I mentioned in Chapter 2. The buyers and retailers I interviewed were fully aware of this growth gap and the increasing need for them to work with smaller manufacturers. They see the unique opportunity small companies have, and they want in. These facts should be used as leverage in your buyer presentations.

Question 15: How important is a supplier's ability to produce private label brands to you?

Buyers and retailers believed that partnerships between themselves and the manufacturers they work with begin and develop in many ways, and that the private label option is often an important factor. As one interviewee said, "a true partnership should go beyond the branded product you offer." That said, you should think about your willingness and ability to produce private label brands.

Question 16: What are some of your top buying priorities?

* Food safety
* Sales growth
* Market share
* Corporate goals
* Profits
* Competition
* Shrink and inventory reduction

Question 17: What trends are you focused on for your buying responsibilities?

* Natural and organics
* Locally raised or produced
* Healthy eating
* Meal solutions
* Packaging
* Online ordering/curbside service
* GMO labeling
* Pick 5 products

In general, the buyers and retailers I spoke with generally ranked their priorities and trend preferences in the order listed above. However, we received a lot of overlapping and sometimes contradictory responses. Several times, their answers lined up with regional or national trends. One thing was certain: food safety is the No. 1 priority on everybody's list. Beyond that, each buyer will have their own corporate initiatives, category priorities, and personal goals. Therefore, I'd advise against assuming that natural and/or organics and transparent sourcing and/or labeling will be at the top of your buyer's agenda. The idea here is knowing the trends and how you might be able to capitalize on them, while also talking with your buyer partners about their priorities and their thoughts on the trends.

OTHER GATEWAY OPTIONS

Smaller manufacturers do have other options when it comes to gatekeepers within the supply chain, including brokers and distributors. While I focus on a company's relationship with buyers and retailers throughout this book because they are likely to be your most frequent partners, an understanding of the roles brokers and distributors play is also important. What follows is the analysis of interviews I conducted with these industry insiders.

Brokers

In the food industry, a broker is an independent sales agent who negotiates sales for food producers and manufacturers. Brokers work with buyers as they help sell products to chain wholesalers, retail stores, independent wholesalers, and more. Some of the buyers and retailers I interviewed represent independent or smaller chains that expressed opposition to the use of brokers because they add cost to each transaction. However, some companies utilize brokers because a broker's goal is to drive sales for their clients. Brokers can act as effective middlemen between you and your gatekeepers.

I found that, in general, any brokers you might work with are interested in the same things that buyers and retailers are when they consider partnering with a manufacturer. They want to see that you've done your homework. They want to know what your marketing budget is. They are particularly interested in knowing if you can offer products that are different or innovative. Once they are on board, brokers act as your sales people as they develop working relationships with the buyers/retailers, familiarize themselves with category planograms, and provide product monitoring and upkeep.

Whether you and your company should employ a broker depends on your own sales and marketing prowess as well as the retail operations you wish to partner with. Companies with strong marketing and sales teams might not need a broker. At the same time, while many mid-sized retail chains prefer that you don't use a broker, many larger chains all but require a broker because some categories require constant attention.

Distributors

A food service distributor is a company that provides food and non-food products to smaller, mid-sized, and independent grocery stores and supermarket chains, as well as restaurants, cafeterias, industrial caterers, hospitals, and nursing homes. The distributor purchases, stores, sells, and delivers those products, providing retailers and food service operators with access to items from a wide variety of manufacturers.

Distributors are viable supply chain options, but they differ from buyers and retailers in a few fundamental ways. Distributors often deal with large-volume purchases and store products for longer time periods, normally selling them to wholesalers and operators at times and in portions that the wholesalers and operators desire.

The sales chain is different with distributors, too. It's up to the distributors to sell your products to manufacturers, food service operators, and retail outlets, while your marketing efforts should support your brand in the overall marketplace.

Because selling to a distributor offers your company a chance to get your products to a wider variety of retail outlets and individual consumers, it has its obvious advantages. Indirect sales avenues such as distributors can act as partners with established markets and proven experience. However, there are also obstacles. Many distributors aren't necessarily brand loyal. Some I talked to also showed a reluctance to partner with smaller manufacturers and unfamiliar companies. Because their sales forces frequently work on 100-percent commission, they sometimes won't even talk to an unfamiliar company.

Still, the distributors I spoke to expressed a general willingness to work with unique local manufacturers. Another option is to do an end-run on a reluctant distributor, which I've seen happen before. Originally snubbed by a distributor, one of NewPoint's client companies instead sold directly to a retail outlet that normally partnered with that distributor. Once the retailer decided to place the product, the distributor was all but forced to begin buying and stocking the product. It's what is called "getting on the truck," which is always a good thing.

CONCLUSION

Whatever their title, your buyers, retailers, brokers, and distributors are the gatekeepers of the food industry, and are crucial to growth and success in the food industry. They represent your ground-zero customers, whereas the end-line consumers are in many ways your customer's customer. Your buyers and retailers must be viewed as potential partners in a mutually beneficial long-term relationship, while brokers can be viewed as third-party middlemen who can be useful but might come with some drawbacks. Distributors represent a different avenue for distribution, but they ultimately want the same things as everyone else. They want a unique, innovative, and opportunistic company that is looking to grow.

Chapter 4

MARKETING IS EVERYTHING

> *"Because it is its purpose to create a customer, any business enterprise has two—and only these two—basic functions: marketing and innovation."*
>
> —Peter Drucker, management consultant, educator, and author

Eight years ago, before he was a client, Rob laid out the situation. Sales were good, but margins were not. His company was stuck selling at wholesale and commodity pricing. Rob went on to say that he felt developing his company's small retail brand was key to growing margins. We explored it, took baby budget steps, and the rest—including three-plus years of more than 100 percent growth—is history.

It wasn't easy to get there. Successful growth takes vision and commitment from a client's entire team. It also helped that, at the time, my NewPoint team had over 30 years of food-industry marketing experience to draw on to drive Rob's plan for brand growth.

What you have in your hands right now is a marketing book, and I'm in the marketing business. That said, my team and I believe that branding and marketing are equally as important as the ingredients in your product.

For example, Kellogg's famously bought Pringles for $2.7 billion, but not because they wanted the uniform chip-making machines that create the uniquely shaped chips uniquely. No, Kellogg's bought Pringles for several reasons, including its brand equity and standing in the growing snack food category. Most of all, however, Kellogg's bought Pringles because of what Rob was alluding to a few paragraphs back: brand = margins.

It stands to reason that, unless you buy into and embrace the notion that marketing needs to be a core component of your business, this book might not be for you. Because we believe that marketing is everything.

The statement, "Marketing is everything", was famously stated by Regis McKenna in the *Harvard Business Review* in 1991, and that declaration is becoming more accurate every day. With the onset of the digital age and the resulting onslaught of 24-7 information flow, marketing has only become more ubiquitous in our society. I will discuss all things marketing related in the upcoming chapters, including brand reconnaissance, brand advantage strategies, brand growth programs, and general brand management programs. My goal is to help you turn your insight into action—and profit.

What follows is a brief introduction to NewPoint's philosophy and processes regarding the fundamentals of marketing. This introduction lays the foundation as well as acts as an overview of the topics I'll address as we move forward.

Please note: For the sake of moving expediently through these chapters, I'm going to assume that your product is already a finished one. This means that it's already fully developed, market-ready, regulation- and requirement-met, and has been previously sold in the market in some capacity.

MARKETING VS. BRANDING VS. ADVERTISING

Before I get too far into the discussion on the aspects of marketing as it applies to your company, it's important that we all get on the same page about the meaning of and relationship between marketing, branding, and advertising. Because these three terms are all related to the sales side of your company's operation, they are often intermingled and/or confused with each other. However, each performs their own distinct functions toward the same goals and fall under the marketing umbrella. Simply put, advertising and branding are both important elements of your company's marketing process, working in unison to establish, enhance, and build equity to your company's reputation and increase sales.

Marketing

Marketing is a process that involves all the strategies, tactics, and activities your company utilizes to build awareness and facilitate the sales of its products and/or services. Marketing acts as the umbrella that encompasses brand, advertising, and anything that brings your products and/or services together with your consumers. This includes websites, social media interactions, printed materials, television and radio promotions, public interactions, and customer service.

To emphasize the importance of marketing as it encompasses branding and advertising, let's look at *Tried and Tasted: The Ultimate Shopping List*, a BBC channel 4 television show hosted by Chef Michel Roux Jr. On each episode, a small panel of food experts blind-taste test Britain's favorite foods, ranging from meat and cheese to crackers to soda and beer, and then they declare taste-test winners. When stripped of their strategically branded packaging, often the most expensive products do not win. Do you think Pringles would win in a blind-taste test against every chip on the market?

The blind-taste testing on *Tried and Tested* is the ultimate testimony to the dazzling sophistication and psychological impact that the marketing of food brands has on our affinity, loyalty, and associations to some brands.

The best illustration of this, of course, is a recent update to the famous blind-taste test that compared Coke and Pepsi. In the blind-taste test, people chose Pepsi over Coke. However, when showed the cans, those same people said they preferred Coke. This is what Barry Smith, Professor of Philosophy at London University, had to say in his updated study of the tests, "That's because they prefer the Coca-Cola brand. There were neuroimaging versions of this test showing that we get pleasure from the brand, activating our pleasure centers. These can influence how we perceive the taste and flavor."

That's a pretty good argument for the Kellogg's purchase of the Pringles brand—which will probably never win a taste test—and proof that marketing is everything.

Brand

According to the American Marketing Association, the official definition of a brand is anything that helps convince potential buyers to remain loyal to your product or company, such as your logo, symbol, name, or design. As I mentioned previously, powerful branding can even triumph over product taste. Brand *is* the message. It's the foundational touchstone that all marketing efforts utilize to build brand equity. Brand equity is often part of a brand's valuation, so dollars are attached to a brand's worth. Branding is what your company believes in, why it exists, and how consumers experience it. Your brand ultimately aligns your company's core ideals with the desires and beliefs of your customers. I'll dig deeper into branding, from brand positioning to brand message to brand promise, starting in Chapter 7.

Advertising

Advertising is the act of delivering a message to a target audience. Advertising focuses specifically on driving sales or gaining customers for your company's products and/or services. The goal of advertising is to get the word out about your product/service through paid campaigns, which are expressly written and designed to reach your target market through various media outlets. I'll cover campaigns, media, and marketing plan development in Chapters 10 through 12.

MARKETING IS EVERYTHING

I've already described marketing as any strategy that helps your company build brand awareness and bring your brand together with customers through all appropriate media outlets. There are four basic steps to developing an effective marketing strategy, including:

1. Know your audience and the competition.
2. Develop a brand that is relevant to your audience, and relative to the competition.
3. Build brand awareness and incentivize its purchase.
4. Monitor and analyze your progress.

While there is a myriad of ways to implement this general strategy, I approach it through the interwoven stages of reconnaissance, advantage strategies, growth programs, and ongoing management.

In upcoming chapters, I'll discuss brand reconnaissance, which I consider to be the first step towards developing a company's effective marketing strategy. I'll also cover how to internally assess your company's plans and goals, perform an external analysis of your industry and your category, as well as how to track of macro and micro trends within your marketplace. A discussion of brand advantage strategies follows, including all the facets of the foundational brand development process. I'll then address brand growth programs, including brand activation, building a regional powerhouse, business-to-business channel strategies, sales and service expansion, and loyalty programs. Finally, I'll end with a discussion on public relations and crisis management, strategic product development, and brand extension strategies.

Marketing Myths Busted

Just as there's frequent confusion between branding, marketing, and advertising, there are also many popular misunderstandings about marketing that can leave business owners like yourself disillusioned. Here is a list of some of those marketing myths, drawn both from personal experience and common industry knowledge, along with the facts that debunk them:

Marketing is expensive. No matter what your budget is, you do have marketing options. If done properly, marketing can help you reach your target market for less money than you think. Also, if your competition is utilizing marketing strategies, can you afford not to use marketing strategies?

Marketing is complicated. In our world, marketing is a manageable process—a scalable, adjustable, and collaborative process.

Marketing is only for big business. The rise of digital media and other creative marketing avenues has made it easier and often less expensive than ever to reach your audience. The creation of a powerful brand message is your most crucial investment.

Marketing is more art than science. This is a myth for people who don't like math. Numbers don't lie, and a good analysis leads to accuracy and cost efficiency. Everything must be measured and evaluated.

Being first matters most. Market timing and the ability to achieve the right fit between your product and the market matter far more than being first. The trick is in finding that fit, which is where a strategic marketing program comes into play.

Competing with the Big Brands

With their huge budgets and mass-market media buys, big brands make marketing appear easy. However, that national reach comes at an enormous cost. According to a 2017 report by businessinsider.com, General Mills spends more than $1 billion annually for advertising, and other food industry giants like the Kraft Foods Group, Inc., aren't far behind. However, remember that big advertising budgets don't necessarily equal market share, which I covered the decline in the previous chapter, nor does category dominance necessarily equal profitability. Gaining market share and increasing margins aren't necessarily the result of more marketing. They're the result of effective marketing and a partnership with an informed sales team.

The nature of the food industry marketplace is undergoing a consumer-driven shift—one that increasingly disdains national advertising efforts. You can take advantage of this change by positioning your company as the antithesis of the big brands by being smaller, familiar, authentic, and transparent. Becoming a powerhouse brand in your chosen region is perhaps your first step as your company grows. Reaching regional powerhouse status, though, depends on your ability to establish that position in the first place. I'll address the process of becoming a regional powerhouse at length later in this book. The complicated relationship between market share and profitability as well as the importance of brand equity will also be covered.

According to a 1997 report by the *Harvard Business Review*, market share alone doesn't drive profitability among premium food product brands. Instead, a brand's profitability is driven by both its market share and the nature of its category. Once you understand your brand's category, you can differentiate it and increase the perceived value—or brand equity—of your product through various marketing techniques. It has been proven by numerous upscale brands across categories that consumers are willing to pay more for the level of quality or prestige attached to brands with a high level of brand equity.

Turning Insight into Action

Before you and your company can implement your brand's marketing platform, first you must do the groundwork that justifies it. It's imperative that you fully understand your company and its place within the broader food-industry marketplace before acting. Doing your homework is extremely important, and it begins with a lot of discovery and even more research. In addition, you must also develop brand strategies for growth and become brand-tactical.

Doing Your Homework

Your homework should begin with both internal and external assessments, with the balance of your internal plan comprising of the "yin" to the "yang" of external forces. Together, this is what we refer to as brand reconnaissance.

Internally, your company needs not only a vision, but also a stated mission and a specific set of plans and goals. In the next section I'll address all the reasons why making plans and setting goals is not only something you should want to do if you plan to grow, but also something you absolutely must do simply to survive. I'll also lay out a comprehensive set of guidelines for planning and goal-setting from proper strategies to avoidable pitfalls.

There's an almost endless amount of information at your disposal when it comes to external analysis, including everything from all-encompassing industry research to old-fashioned store checks. Your homework should include, among other things, quantitative and qualitative market research designed to complete the analysis of your industry, category, and competition. Quantitative methods emphasize objective measurements and statistical analysis of data; including IRI/Infoscan and Nielsen data, in-person store checks, and strategically chosen industry associations; with the goal of understanding how your company fits into the overall marketplace landscape. Qualitative methods, which often consist of interviews and/or focus groups, are meant to uncover trends in the thoughts and opinions of consumers. For the purposes of your company, it should include interviews with the following: retail stores that already partner with you, retail stores that don't partner with you, your peers and other role players in your food supply chain, industry researchers, and innovators, and finally, consumers.

The combination of your internal and external assessments will ultimately help you determine where you fit into the marketplace. Crucial information, such as cost structure, projected growth, projected profitability, entry barriers, distribution methods, and key success factors, will be revealed. I'll discuss all of this and more in the upcoming chapters.

Brand Development

All the internal and external work in brand reconnaissance mentioned previously is an important building block for brand development and growth. It begins with the creation of a compelling brand story that effectively positions your brand in relation to the competition. Instead of being like other options on the shelf, which industry insiders refer to as a "me, too" product, a good brand story should be one that differentiates your brand and enhances your relevance by being unique and exceptional. Further development consists of the formation of a comprehensive strategy that is designed to create brand awareness, invite brand engagement, and grow your brand. Later, I'll lay out specific ways to identify and write out key components of your branded product and discuss the differences between branding and brand positioning. I'll also address the importance of creating a brand message, incorporating a brand promise, and developing a consistent visual brand identity within your strategy for growth. These factors are important for the creation of a direct relationship between your company, its brand, and the consumer.

Brand Tactical Development

Once the foundational research and brand strategies are completed, it's time for the final step: getting brand-tactical to increase awareness of your brand and initiate sales at retail outlets. This involves the identification and creation of channel strategies, which includes business-to-business sales strategies for food service, retail, and distributors; trade shows; displays and sales support materials; and customer cultivation. Getting brand-tactical also means creating branded packaging, developing co-packing and/or private label relationships with your distributors, and creating a marketing plan with brand-integrated campaigns and promotions. These marketing campaigns should be designed to increase brand awareness and invite trial and engagement, often through grassroots strategies. The marketing plan should also include a creative digital marketing program. I'll cover all of this as we proceed.

CONCLUSION

When your food industry research and brand strategies are completed, it's time for the final step: getting brand-tactical to increase awareness of your brand. It involves the identification and creation of channel strategies—strategies that begin with a vision and a lot of homework and end with a first-class brand that can dominate its region and compete with Big Food on store shelves wherever you choose. Marketing obviously isn't the only thing your company should focus on, but marketing can mean everything. Buy into it.

Section 2

Brand Reconnaissance

Chapter 5

INTERNAL PLANS AND GOALS

"I've always been in the right place and time. Of course, I steered myself there."

—Bob Hope, entertainer

"If you don't know where you are going, any road will get you there."

—Lewis Carroll, author

It has already been mentioned that for you and your brand to become successful, you must do a lot of homework. Rest assured—the homework assignments will come. For now, we are going to hit you with a pop quiz.

Question 1: What are the names of two customers you aspire to work with?

Question 2: What is your plan for adding those customers to your list of current partners?

Your answer to Question 1 is important, of course, but it's also sort of a trick question because the only answer that really matters comes in Question 2: What is your plan? The word *plan* is obviously the operative word here, and that one word can make the difference between success and failure when it comes to the sustained growth of your company and its brand.

At first, I was on the fence about even including a chapter about planning and goal setting in this book. My original thought was that it seems obvious whoever is bothering to read this book likely has set goals for growing their product long ago. However, after decades in the marketing business, I've spoken with numerous business owners who've come to NewPoint for assistance—be it a new website, a packaging change, a branded promotional project, or something else—and their plan was only to sell and then sell more. That's it.

One of the first questions NewPoint asks business owners who come to us with a project is: "What are the overall goals that you are trying to achieve, and how does this project fit into those goals?" Often, there's no concrete answer. If there is one, it tends to be reactionary in nature. Maybe they've invested in a new processing machine for their factory floor and want to get busy using it. Perhaps they want to update their packaging, advertising, website, or social media platforms so that those programs are up to par with their competition? Whatever their reasons for contacting us, we rarely see strategy behind their decision, which can be a mistake.

In this chapter, I discuss setting your plans and goals in stone. After first addressing in-depth the reasons why it's important to plan and set goals, I'll present you with a template for how you plan and finish utilizing examples of companies that succeeded because of their effective planning and goal-setting.

WHY MAKE PLANS?
Plan Because You Want To

One thing that I've learned through both personal and client experience is that while a good salesperson might be able to get your product on the shelf, only a team with vision and a solid plan can drive your product's market share. The goals for both you and your retailers is increased market share and, in turn, profits.

Having a solid business plan, one that sets concrete goals towards manageable future growth, means planning for change. If there's one thing that's certain in business, it's change. Within the fluid environment of your marketplace, Darwinian principles will decide the difference between the winners and the losers. Companies that resist change or cannot keep up will, at best, be stuck treading water and become stagnant. In the worst-case scenario, these companies will lose their market share or fail outright. In short, companies that do not or refuse to evolve are in danger of eventually becoming less relevant and possibly going extinct. In the case of a smaller, regional, or local food manufacturer like yourself, change is good.

As I discussed in a previous chapter, recent history has shown that Big Food was perfectly happy to rest on decades' worth of success and enjoy the enormous market share that success brought, only to see its status threatened by change. In just a few short years, the heavy hitters have begun losing the growth game to aggressive local and regional food brands like yours. Most of these aggressors found themselves in the right place at the right time on purpose. They saw the opportunity that came with change, made a solid plan, and filled a niche in the marketplace. That niche is growing.

Plan Because You Should
The Numbers

Goal-setting might sound yet another way to waste paper and fill your conference room with hot air, but nothing could be further from the truth. A startling number of companies fail, in part, because they lacked an effective goal-setting strategy. Furthermore, yours isn't the only local, smaller, or regional food manufacturing company fighting for room in this evolving marketplace.

Here's a list of statistics related to small businesses and their failure, according to a 2014 msn.com article:

* Generally, the Small Business Administration states that new businesses have about a 40 percent chance of surviving for five or more years.
* According to the National Federation of Independent Businesses, only 39 percent of small businesses prove to be profitable over their lifetime.
* The *Harvard Business Review* and *Business Now* magazine both cite lack of planning among the top five reasons small businesses fail, with the *Harvard Business Review* ranking it No. 2.
* A 2014 University of Tennessee study named general incompetence, which included lack of planning, as its runaway No. 1 reason for failure. The study found that incompetence was the reason for failure a whopping 49 percent of the time.

Scary, right? Well, it gets worse. What follows is a list of frequently cited statistics related to overall strategy—known as planning and goal-setting—culled from the research of strategic management experts Robert Kaplan and David Norton:

* Nine out of 10 companies fail to execute strategy.
* Only 25 percent of managers have incentives linked to strategy.
* Only 5 percent of the workforce understands their company's strategy.
* Only 15 percent of executive teams spend more than one hour per month discussing strategy. Again, that's one hour per month. In contrast, a 2015 *Forbes* article found that 31 percent of company employees typically spend an hour per day on Facebook.

Alarmingly, most small companies hardly do any planning at all. Lack of planning is one of the main reasons why most small companies fail. Therefore, in many ways, survival of the fittest means survival of most goal-oriented and strategically prepared.

The Competition

Yours isn't the only local, small, or regional company hoping to take advantage of the volatile nature of today's food industry marketplace. According to a 2017 report compiled jointly by the USDA and Mintel's Global New Product Database, the number of food and beverage product introductions in retail outlets is likely to generally continue to grow for the foreseeable future. Among their findings were the following facts:

* New U.S. food and beverage product introductions in retail outlets have followed a general upward trend since the late 1990s.
* In 2016, the number of new food and beverage product introductions reached their highest level since 2007.
* The number of new food and beverage product introductions increased 25 percent between 2015 and 2016.

This report also suggested that your competition is trying to grow the same way you are—by capitalizing on the evolving consumer tastes and preferences we discussed in Chapter 1. Among the claims made on the packaging of all the new products introduced in 2016, health-related attributes accounted for 7 of the top 10 claim categories. At least a few of your competitors know what they are doing. Shouldn't you?

INTENTIONAL SUCCESS

What does success mean for your company? Would you like to double your sales volume in two years? Do you want to increase your margins by 10 points on key product lines? How about reducing lead times by two days or being more flexible with fill rates? One way to guarantee success is to ensure your entire team is involved in deciding what success is, then engaging in supporting the effort.

Successful companies, including those in the food industry, set goals. Plan creation and goal setting helps define a company's purpose and provides benchmarks to measure success. Companies that don't set goals tend to struggle, failing to reach meaningful accomplishments, and stagnating. In your industry where change is increasingly driving the marketplace, stagnation is the enemy. Just ask the heavy hitters how true this is.

A concrete and achievable set of goals must be part of your business plan as you prepare to battle Big Food and increase your market share. Goals must become a regular part of your ongoing business operations. What follows is a simple, yet crucial, set of guidelines for setting your company's goals.

Perform a SWOT Analysis

One common method many companies utilize to analyze their business is what's known as SWOT analysis. SWOT stands for strengths, weaknesses, opportunities, and threats, and a SWOT analysis assesses these factors. Strengths and weaknesses represent internal factors, while opportunities and threats represent external factors.

Strengths: What are your company's strongest attributes? What makes it different from the competition?

Weaknesses: How does your company need to improve to remain competitive?

Opportunities: Which external factors can you identify that might give your company a competitive advantage?

Threats: Which external factors have the potential to do your business harm?

Performing a SWOT analysis is an effective way to reveal both the good and the bad aspects of you company, and can help you focus as you develop your business plan. This analysis should be simple, specific, and realistic, and you should be careful not to overanalyze.

Create a Vision Statement

A vision statement is an articulation of your company's aspirational goals. It should describe what you and your company are trying to build and provide an ideological touchstone for future actions. Your vision might be to see your brand on the shelves of every grocery store you walk into or to have it on every restaurant table you sit at. While it isn't a part of your company's strategic road map to success, your vision statement should answer the question, "Where do we want to go?" Ultimately, your vision should be your inspiration.

Create a Mission Statement

While your vision statement should focus on your company's future, your mission statement should be a brief description of your company's fundamental purpose in its present state. It should answer the question, "Why does our company exist?" An effective mission statement broadly describes your company's present capabilities, customer focus, activities, and overall business makeup. Unlike your vision statement, which is normally an internal company document, your mission statement is intended to be a part of your company's public face. As such, it should be drafted with your company's marketing and advertising programs in mind.

Wishes Are Not Goals

While writing a vision statement is important, they are just declarative statements of your wishes and dreams. "My company is going to make more money" is a wish. So is "My company is going to become a regional food industry powerhouse." To transform your wishes into goals, you and your company must design a specific strategic plan that includes concrete goals. An effective strategic plan considers all the things your business can and should do based on its strengths and weaknesses, helping you to determine where to spend your time and money. There are hundreds of strategic planning resources out there to choose from, and each company develops its own style of plan. My advice is to find a plan that suits you or work with a consultant to do so. Otherwise, what you thought were goals likely will become a little more than pipe dreams.

Strategic is SMART

One popular procedure for setting goals goes by the acronym SMART, which stands for specific, measurable, attainable, relevant, and time-sensitive:

Specific: You have defined what you want to accomplish.

Measurable: You have identified targets and milestones.

Attainable: Your goal is realistic and manageable.

Relevant: Your goal fits into your overall business model.

Time-Sensitive: You have set a timeframe for the goal's accomplishment.

Using this simple and time-tested method of goal setting encourages you and your company to be more efficient and productive. It helps you to break down your goals into validated segments, track your progress, and keep an eye on both the bigger picture and day-to-day details.

Goals as Stepping Stones

Simply put, goals are resolutions to achieve a desired result. Both short-term goals and long-term goals provide a clear understanding of what your company is striving to accomplish. Set short-term goals, such as incremental reductions in lead times, as stepping stones to encourage everyone as they strive to meet the long-term goals. Having goals gives everybody's everyday tasks increased meaning and clarifies the reasoning behind your company's decisions.

Spread the Word

It's important that your goals are written out and disseminated within your company. You should also map out the methods you plan to use in attaining each goal. Remember, the present nature of the food industry is evolving, so your goals are bound to change along the way. Welcome and embrace that change, but be mindful that you do not abandon your overall goals as you proceed.

Set Team Goals

Your company is ultimately a team of individuals who share a common vision—success through growth. As such, everyone on the team, from individuals to specific departments and upward, should have concrete goals. Maybe you want a new item developed to increase your stock keeping unit (SKUs), or maybe you want to streamline production to reduce lead time? Your goals should encompass every aspect of your company's overall strategy, from initial development to production to the final sale and fulfillment of orders. The result is a true team effort, a camaraderie that boosts morale and produces a sense of responsibility as you transform your shared goals into reality. Involving all your employees in the goal-setting and implementation process also ensures that the goals you set are realistic and attainable.

Keep Setting Goals

Do not think of goal-setting as a one-time event that takes place only when you develop your initial business plan. All markets change, and the food industry marketplace is evolving more than ever right now. Savvy owners of local, small, and regional companies—owners like you—must take advantage of each situation as the market evolves. Having a solid foundation of concrete goals will help you get off the ground, gain momentum as you grow, and even maintain that momentum should you encounter a slump.

Avoid Pitfalls

Clearly, there are many things you should do while you're setting goals, and several things you should NOT do. To make your goal-setting process as efficient as possible, here are a few common goal-setting mistakes you should try to avoid:

Waiting for the perfect time to start. Resist the urge to procrastinate or feel overwhelmed.

Failing the S.M.A.R.T. test. Efficiency is crucial, and you know the method. Use it.

Being inflexible. Remain open to changes during the process of achieving your goals.

Not working on your goals daily. It's easy to set and forget goals, but they require constant attention and frequent adjustments.

Forgetting to celebrate success. Acknowledging incremental milestones helps you build momentum.

CONCLUSION

It's an unfortunate fact of life that small businesses, including those in the food industry, fail more often than they succeed. It's more unforgivable than unfortunate, however, that one of the primary reasons small businesses fail is lack of planning. Don't be that business. Create a comprehensive business plan that includes attainable goals. Transform your vision into a mission, develop a strategic implementation plan, act on that plan regularly, and involve your whole team. Together, you can achieve success.

Chapter 6

EXTERNAL MARKET FACTORS

"All suppliers should be experts. Unfortunately, they are not. You need to be prepared. You need to know your product and the competition. If you don't know your product or the competition, you are never going to win."

—M. L., category buyer, 16 years' experience

The prospect of doing homework that involves number crunching and analysis might seem both unpleasant and daunting. But make no mistake about it, as you, your company, and its brand strive to move up the food chain, all that tedious homework can turn you into a killer within your category. And, a killer is exactly what you must become when you go after the big fish.

The big fish in your world are all members of Big Food, and they are the apex predators in the food chain of both the food industry in general and your product category in particular. Everyone knows who they are, and it's always a good idea to keep an eye on what they are up to. However, for most local, small, or regional companies such as yours, moving up the food chain is an incremental process that includes a series of small victories over vulnerable opponents. For you, it may mean identifying the weakest competitor in your category, displacing them, and then locating your next prey.

In short, if you want to climb up the food chain, you must become a meticulous and calculating predator. This killer instinct should always exist during your company's planned growth, from original project development through the process of dominating your own backyard and becoming a regional powerhouse.

Becoming meticulous and calculating—becoming a killer—requires you adopt a new perspective that focuses on where you, your company, and its brand fit into the surrounding competitive environment. This is called external analysis, and it comprises the "yang" to the "yin" of your internal assessment, which we discussed in a previous chapter. Together, the internal and external assessments determine where your product stands within its category as well as its market share. Understanding your true standing in the marketplace helps you decide which of your opponents should be vanquished next.

External analysis consists of quantitative analysis and qualitative analysis. Quantitative methods, which typically consist of polls, questionnaires, and/or surveys, emphasize objective measurements of statistics and the analysis of data within a given category. In our case, there's no shortage of food industry research and data in every category that can be acquired for external analysis. Qualitative analysis, which often consists of consumer focus groups and interviews with important industry insiders, is meant to uncover trends and the thoughts and opinions of consumers.

Your execution of a comprehensive external analysis goes a long way toward your goal of becoming an expert in your category, which is an absolute necessity as you attempt to make fruitful connections with your buyers as well as your end-line consumers. Buyers love to work with experts, but the buyers I interviewed for this book often found their suppliers' knowledge lacking. Your buyers have access to much of the same information as you do, so they know which suppliers have done their homework and those who have not. Don't be that supplier.

Our buyers also voice disdain for "me-too" products, which they described as items that are otherwise indistinguishable from other products that they see daily and are likely to be already on store shelves. When it comes to choosing between your brand and all the other products available in your category, particularly a product buyers already carry, they will be looking for reasons why they should go with yours. An expert with killer instincts has those reasons readily at hand.

IN THEIR OWN WORDS:
Buyers on the Importance of Expertise

> "I think it's important that suppliers understand what's going on in your stores, as well as the competition. For instance, if they are there to pitch a new item, they should already know, are there other items (like theirs) in the category? Who are the brands? How's it doing in the market? Sometimes I would get rather agitated when someone sat down in front of me and didn't have an answer to any of these questions."
>
> —C. F., senior buyer, 27 years' experience

> "I can't imagine a vendor not being a 100-percent expert with their products. If they are producing it and spending all their revenue and square feet to produce a product, you're going to want to be an expert in this product."
>
> —T. P., category manager, 21 years' experience

Moving on to quantitative methods, qualitative methods, and effective trend research, let's look at aspects of category and market analysis, including overall size, projected growth, profitability, entry barriers, cost structure, distribution systems, and key success factors. An understanding of these factors, which comprise the technological, governmental, cultural, and economic facets of the food industry, is crucial if even the smallest of companies expects to survive and thrive in its competitive environment.

Quantitative Research

In the case of external food industry analysis at least, the numbers don't lie. Neither does information from select industry insiders and an old-fashioned eye test. By utilizing IRI-category data purchases, Nielsen research, reports from strategically chosen industry associations, as well as in-person store checks, you can begin to fully understand the scope and scale of your marketplace's competitive landscape. It's important for you to incorporate frequent analysis of these factors into your normal operational habits so that you remain informed, please your buyers, and proactively address consumer and industry trends.

IRI

The IRI website proclaims that, as one of the original innovators in Big Data, it integrates the world's largest set of otherwise disconnected purchase, media, social, casual, and loyalty data with the goal of helping consumer package goods companies, among others, grow their business. IRI combines data with predictive analytics to uncover new consumer insights that can help you gain leverage in your marketplace. Among other things, IRI offers marketing performance reviews, strategy solutions, deep shopper insights, activation strategies, and media solutions.

Nielsen

On its website, Nielsen touts itself as a global leader in retail measurement services by offering purchasing data that is comprehensive and timely. Nielsen's aim is to arm companies with actionable and holistic intelligence through flexible analytics. The company provides information on market shares and competitive sales volumes, as well as insights into distribution, pricing, merchandising, and promotion with the goal of helping companies improve their manufacturing, marketing, and sales decisions.

Industry Associations

Industry associations, by definition, support and protect the rights of industries and the people who work in them. Every industry, including the food industry, has numerous associations. Once you've become a member, your industry association(s) basically act as lobbying groups for your category. They also help you distill IRI and Nielsen analysis, keep up with industry reports, and track consumer trends. A simple Wikipedia search for "list of food industry trade associations" will point you in the direction of many associations you might be interested in joining, from the American Cheese Society to the World Apple and Pear Association and beyond.

In-Person Store Checks

While IRI, Nielsen, and industry associations can provide you and your company with crucial outside information based on data and analysis, in-person store checks represent your very personal evaluation of the state of your category. Store checks are where theory meets reality on the shelves of every retail store you currently team with as well as those you hope to team with in the future. It's my belief that you can learn much more by seeing your competitive market firsthand than you can with just the numbers, and that your store checks should be conducted frequently.

A good store check performs a full SKU count in the category planogram, which is the retail set of products within each category. It also takes note of all competitive brands and their share within the planogram, their product's features or flavoring, pricing, packaging innovation, and shopper marketing—basically everything about all products on the shelf. In short, a good store check involves understanding the competition within the planogram and identifying those SKUs you wish to displace.

Qualitative Research

While most quantitative analysis involves data-driven research of your marketplace, qualitative analysis is usually aimed at discovering the thoughts, opinions, and motivations of your consumers, retail partners, and food industry insiders. Qualitative research normally involves a relatively small sample size and can be accomplished with a relatively small budget. According to widely accepted industry opinions of best practices standards, qualitative research often includes the utilization of focus groups, participation observation, individual interviews, and surveys, among other methods. The aim is to establish an initial understanding of your primary target audience's psychographics, feelings, beliefs, and viewpoints about things associated with your product and the competitive field. Everything from a brand's name and packaging to a product's look and advertising can be considered—all in the name of establishing a sound base for further marketing and product development decision making. Following are a few types of qualitative research methods that you can utilize to procure the information you need:

Focus groups. Engage a small group of people (usually 6-10) who share a common set of characteristics (demographics, attitudes, etc.) in a moderated trial-and-discussion session about your product, your brand, and/or your company.

Individual interviews. Talk privately with individual focus group members or other respondents to gain their unique and in-depth perspectives.

Participation observation. Watch consumer behavior in real-world settings without any attempt to manipulate their actions.

Surveys. Engage in specifically designed telephone surveys and customer satisfaction surveys to acquire information you need.

There are several instances where you'll want to utilize these qualitative research methods, beginning with new product ideation and development to brand positioning and marketing strategy. Qualitative research will also help you discover the strengths and weaknesses of your company and its brand, understand the dynamics of purchasing, and explore specific market segments.

Because it's ultimately the end-line consumers who are buying or not buying your brand, they should be the primary target for your qualitative research. Often, the end-line consumer is a mom because statistics say that she's still the decision-maker when it comes to food purchases. However, it's also important to include other food industry insiders in your research. They include retail store operators you partner with, retail store operators you don't partner with, your peers, and other significant players in the food supply and service chain, as well as industry researchers, innovators. and thought leaders.

Capitalizing on Trends

Enterprising food industry companies NewPoint talks to tend to be entrepreneurial, and trends in consumer behavior and industry dynamics represent opportunities for you and your company. A company's flexibility and willingness to change offers a potential advantage over both the slower-moving big brands and less-competitive small companies in your marketplace. Therefore, it's therefore in your best interest to remain dialed in to current and future trends taking place within your complex and ever-changing marketplace. That said, it's imperative that you know which trends to pay attention to, how to cross-reference them for validity, and how to use them to your advantage.

Tracking Trends

Trends come in two basic varieties: macro trends and micro trends. Macro trends are overarching tendencies in consumer behavior, such as an increasing preference for healthy and convenient alternatives. Micro trends are fast-moving, ever-changing, and often elusive shifts in tastes that take place within the overall macro trends. A small or mid-sized company that is hoping to grow its brand needs to track both types of trends.

Macro Trends

As I wrote this book, there were five major macro trends at work in the evolving food industry, including consumer preferences for healthy eating, locally sourced and produced products, meal solutions, online ordering/curbside service, and sustainable packaging. Within healthy eating, the biggest trends are consumer preferences for natural and/or organic products. As I've previously shown, these trends have been active for some time and promise to become increasingly important in the future. It's up to you to determine how you to leverage one or more of these trends to gain an edge and increase your SKU presence on store shelves.

Micro Trends

Micro trends change quickly in today's food world. With limitless information and seemingly endless choices, "the next big thing" and "the new super food" come along almost every day. As I wrote this book, some popular micro trends included food service in grocery stores, home-delivered meal kits, and micro or small-batch products. You need to follow these micro trends because there's always a chance that your company can quickly capitalize on one or more of them. Furthermore, it's important to track these trends closely so that you can separate real trends from mere fads, and therefore ensure that you are hunting strategically rather than expending energy without much return.

Trend Resources

There are several go-to resources for trend research in the food industry, beginning with the Food Marketing Institute, Deloitte, and the Grocery Manufacturers Association. Industry publications such as *Supermarket News, Progressive Grocer, Food Business News,* and *Food*

Processing are also useful, as are many more publications like them. Finally, as previously discussed, your chosen industry association(s) are also good resources for trends that are specific to your products.

Your Gatekeepers and Trends

As the gatekeepers of your food world, your buyers or retailers love trends almost as much as they love suppliers who are experts. I've discussed all the trends mentioned previously with numerous gatekeepers for this book, and those discussions led to the following three general conclusions:

* Capitalizing on trends is good for business.
* Local, small, and regional companies have an advantage when it comes to trends.
* Healthy eating in general is the most important current trend.

The fact that capitalizing on trends is good for business is really a no-brainer. As the consumer-driven marketplace continues to evolve and options continue to diversify, those that identify and leverage these trends are the winners at the check-out counter. Nothing makes a buyer or retailer happier than moving products.

The buyers and retailers I spoke with generally saw the benefits of working with small and mid-sized companies like yours in terms of capitalizing on trends. They believe that because your company is smaller and more ambitious than the competition makes you more likely to experiment, evolve, and innovate as you grow. Your flexibility stands in stark contrast to the deeply entrenched strategies and general inertia of your Big Food competitors. In the eyes of the buyers and retailer I spoke to, buying local was itself an important trend. As I've mentioned earlier and will discuss at length later, there are several factors related to consumer preferences that favor local companies and their products. This type of trend naturally favors a company such as yours.

A clear majority of the buyers and retailers I spoke with identified healthy eating in general as the dominant trend in consumer tastes and preferences. While some of them singled out natural/organic foods as the most important healthy eating trend and others favored non-GMO products, almost all of them saw overall healthy eating as the primary trend. The importance of the other trends I mentioned depended largely on geography, consumer demographics, and personal gatekeeper preference.

IN THEIR OWN WORDS:
Buyers on Trend Capitalization

> *"It's important that, when suppliers go in and sit down with a buyer, they can show him what the consumer trends are—this is the demographic that you have to go after, this is the age group that we're looking to capture. Then support it, have all the data, and the information. Once you have that, everything will start to fall together."*
>
> —B. T., senior buyer, 30 years' experience

> *"Having an understanding of all the trends, everything that's going on in the industry, takes a lot of research for a company. All of that is going to help them on all of those initial meetings, or even product development."*
>
> —W. N., senior buyer, 25 years' experience

CONCLUSION

Describing external analysis as a crucial part of the "yin" and "yang" of your company's brand reconnaissance might make it sound peaceful, but it is not. Quantitative research, qualitative research, and trend analysis are designed to hone your skills as a food industry predator. The goal in your quest to grow your business is to identify your competition, determine who is vulnerable, and overtake them. Your prize comes in the form of SKUs, and the more SKUs the better. The next step in your quest is to parlay brand reconnaissance into effective brand development strategies.

Section 3

Brand Advantage Strategies

Chapter 7

FOUNDATIONAL BRAND DEVELOPMENT

The first brand was created to differentiate cows—my cows from your cows. A distinctive, original symbol called a logo was drawn up and bent into an iron stamp. This iron stamp was then heated up and burned into a cow's backside, enabling me to tell my cattle apart from others without confusion. It, then, became easier to keep cattle safe from thieves. It also helped differentiate the livestock when taken to market. The local stockyards where my livestock was sold might give me a better price for my cattle over my competitors. Why? Because the folks there knew my story and trusted that the livestock bearing my logo were taken care of and going to get a great return on resale. In this case, branding a cow is no different than identifying a product. Different companies selling similar products need something to help differentiate from the rest of the "herd."

A Brand Becomes a Story

The history of soap is another good example of how brand can differentiate products. According to *The Advertising Age Encyclopedia of Advertising* by John McDonough and Karen Egolf, making soap was a daily household chore before the Civil War. It's probably safe to say that manufacturing soap on a larger scale was simple and had a very low entry barrier into the marketplace. A new company named Proctor and Gamble (P&G) then started manufacturing soap to supply men in the Union army and, soon after, Colgate-Palmolive introduced its own brand. Competition was born.

By the 1880s, soap led the way in developing mass advertising in the form of newspaper ads and fliers plastered on walls in city streets, handed out door-to-door, and hung in trolley cars. Next came the Industrial Revolution. Mass manufacturing processes made it cheaper to create long runs of product. Railways made it easy for one company to set up a huge soap manufacturing operation and ship their product anywhere.

What did the generic soap manufacturers do? They created reasons to help consumers decide to try their product. They named their soap, developed a logo, and created distinctive and attractive packaging that listed the soap's fine features and qualities and how using it would benefit the user. They also started telling the story of their product. Maybe the soap produced soft beautiful hands. Or maybe consumers learned about the highly skilled craftsmen who spent years developing the perfect soap recipe.

In short, soap manufacturers tried to separate, differentiate, and look like a better choice than the competition.

It was key that each new company stuck to its story and told that story repeatedly in its packaging and advertising. Folks began to recognize the company, know the story, and develop a perception of the product as they saw it on the shelf. Each new soap company wrote the story it wanted people to know about their business and product. What happened to those soap manufacturers who did nothing? Without a branded story, consumers ended up writing their own stories about those companies—good, bad or ugly. Of course, branding today has become an integral component of selling consumer products, including food. It's rare that any company leaves its brand story to chance.

Please note that, as this discussion of brand stories continues, I'll be using big brands and their products as examples often for a couple of reasons. First, big-brand products should be recognizable to everyone who might read this book, making them good example subjects. Furthermore, I've already mentioned that Big Food invests a lot of time, effort, and money into marketing and does some of it very well. There's much to be learned from them, especially when it comes to connecting a brand to an expected experience.

A while back, I bought a box of generic crackers instead of Triscuits. The generic crackers were less expensive and, as I looked at all the options on the store shelf, I wondered, "How can you screw up a cracker?" As a young marketer, I was aware that much of a brand manager's job is to elevate the consumer's perception of the brand they manage. How much of what they say about their brands is true? Does Nabisco really provide a superior cracker? Do I buy in to Nabisco's brand message that my cheese and pepperoni toppings deserve more than the cheapest cracker I can find? I think you know where this is leading. After tasting the dry and flavorless off-brand cracker, I was right back in line, paying a dollar more for the Triscuits I usually buy.

Since the first branded product emerged over a century ago, companies have been honing their brand development skills as well as creating quality products that match the brand promise—a promise they need to make to create a brand preference and command a higher price. That product really needs to be consistently higher in quality and deliver the goods (the brand promise) so that it can command the higher price point and, more importantly, earn the target audience's trust. This, in turn, has led to the next thing that companies excelled at: developing brand affinity with the target audience.

M&M's candy is a good example of a brand meaning something. These chocolate candies have been a consumer favorite since WWII, but the M&M's brand took on special meaning when parent company Mars released presidential M&M's upon the request of President Ronald Reagan in 1988. Patriotically themed boxes of presidential M&M's replaced cigarettes as free gifts on Air Force One that year, and have been given as free gifts to guests of the president ever since. A box of M&M's came to mean more than just chocolate.

The Golden Age of Brand

The Golden Age of Television, which began sometime in the 1940s, brought together the best practices of radio, theater, and filmmaking to create a new form of engaging content fitting the mass market creation called television. The mass market responded by buying televisions and couches, and effectively crowned TV as the dominant form of entertainment that we know today.

Like the early years of television, what we like to call the Golden Age of Brand currently brings together a compelling story of brand, competition, and an audience of consumers who are engaged and willing to play an interactive role. For a brand to survive, it must be bought. At the same time, the Golden Age of Brand has unfolded as name brands have grown across all categories and product segments to a point where we literally interact with brands all day long.

Brands are a part of our lives and, now more than ever, brands are a part of our daily conversations. We all know that the coffee we drink, the smartphones we stare at, and the cars we drive are branded products competing for our loyalty and dollars.

Our current branded culture may have formally started with the Pepsi Challenge in 1975, which became a media sensation centered around the top two warring cola brands. Even though Coke has won over the years, that question of brand loyalty entered the lexicon of our everyday lives. Which do you prefer, Coke or Pepsi? Since then, consumers have been taking sides in brand wars of all kinds—Avis vs. Hertz, Burger King vs. McDonald's, Apple vs. Microsoft (or IBM/Google/Samsung), Bud Lite vs. Miller Lite, Audi vs. BMW, and Verizon vs. AT&T.

As part of all these brand wars, consumers have been introduced to thousands of advertising campaigns and characters over the years that have proven to be conversation topics around the water cooler. Starting with the "I wish I were an Oscar Meyer Wiener" jingle in 1965 and continuing through to the famous "I'd Like to Buy the World a Coke" commercials in the 1970s, the Wendy's "Where's the Beef!" campaign in the 1980s, and Budweiser's "We'll Never Forget" ad commemorating 9/11, there have been many memorable campaigns.

Truly effective and impactful ad campaigns are not only created from the foundation of the brand promise, but they become ingrained in our culture. They are part of our daily lexicon and elevated that brand above its category. For instance, how important and relevant is Nike's "Just Do it"? This campaign, launched in 1988, made such a big impact on the company and category, as well as our popular culture overall, that even today most other athletic brands have basically been reduced to "me-too" brands.

It does not matter if someone likes or owns any of these brands. Even if the public just watches from the sidelines, mass media has elevated brands to the point where they become more than just products we buy. When CNN reports that Apple is worth more than the gross national product (GNP) of Poland, Belgium, Sweden, Saudi Arabia, and Taiwan combined, you can bet that brand news is mainstream news.

What's the role of consumers in all this? Consumers today actively engage and are aware that they are being marketed to. It's part of the dance that has been growing more sophisticated with every ad, billboard, Tweet, Facebook "like", and purchase. Consumers have grown to expect a lot from their brands as they buy their favorite ones from Apple to M&M's to Triscuits and everything in between.

In this section of the book, I'll share the important processes of finding your true brand strength, brand messaging, and brand positioning, among other things. Later chapters within this section will address your company's branded visual voice, branded packaging, and branded campaign elements.

Rules for Brand Positioning

It is one big, crowded, crazy-competitive world out there. How does a brand stand a chance? By finding its true brand strength and focusing on winning. Consider the following as you move ahead.

The Positioning Challenge

The goal of brand positioning is to determine and crystallize a business's single most powerful point of differentiation in the marketplace. Then, the business must use that position as a foundation for all marketing going forward.

For instance, until a few years ago, most supermarkets from independent to mass market all had pretty much the same footprint: a non-differentiated produce section and identical or similar big brands lining the center of the store and freezer cases. Then came Whole Foods, which claimed the position (or what they call a motto) of "Whole Foods, Whole People, Whole Planet", that wrote several supporting statements describing their unique value proposition. Before that, if you wanted organic, natural, or transparent food, you had to either go to a farmer's market or that weird store in your community that smelled like a musty potato bin.

In an overcommunicated marketplace, consumers need clearly defined brands to help them make buying decisions. More than half of the frequently asked questions on the government's nutrition.gov homepage are related to healthier eating. This means a significant market segment is looking for healthier eating alternatives, and Whole Foods grabbed it first, even though the company is relatively new.

Good Brand Positioning Is Sticky

The "Whole Foods = organic and natural foods" brand position has been so strong for so long that natural/organic "sticks" to Whole Foods like an ant in honey. Walmart's "sticky" brand position is low price. The "sticky" position at Starbucks is the expensive premium-coffee experience.

A Brand Position Cannot Be Abstract

To own a good strong position, a brand must be focused, succinct, real, and tangible. This position is easier to find when a company recognizes what they really sell. For instance, Ben & Jerry's does not sell ice cream. Ben & Jerry's sells a progressive social mission in a hippie hat. Similarly, Arby's does not sell fast food. It sells "the meats." Pepsi sells youthful exuberance and not soda. Tropicana does not sell orange juice. It sells Florida sunshine. The sooner a brand dials in on what it really sells, the easier it is to define a tangible brand position.

A Brand Position Must Be Relevant to the Prospect

A brand position must be relevant to the prospect in the way it speaks to something the target audience cares about. Defining an audience is the first and most important step in positioning a brand. The tighter and narrower the focus, the better the chance for success.

For example, first-time parents research every product that having to do with their babies. Just as their cribs, strollers, and baby seats all must be the safest and highest-rated to be considered for purchase, the baby's food must be the best for developmental and cognitive growth. A brand position may be so strong in the market that there is no question of it being bought. For example, Gerber came out with Gerber Organic SmartNourish, a brand name that's essentially synonymous with baby food in the way Xerox is for copying and Google is for internet research. Gerber Organic SmartNourish is a product name that hits all the high notes. In addition, the product delivers. Gerber Organic SmartNourish is listed at the top of *Consumer Reports* stage 1 baby food recommendations.

A Brand Position Must Be Relative to the Competition

It's a brand-eat-brand world in every category. To stand out, a brand position must be relative to every other competitive option. A brand needs to own a position that no one else has. Here are a few examples of slogans that position brands:

* You can "Have it Your Way" at Burger King, as opposed to the strict assembly-line burger you get from McDonald's (as Burger King would have you believe).
* There's a "Pepsi Generation," as opposed to the old folks who like Coke (as the Pepsi-perpetuated myth goes).
* Pork is the "Other White Meat" as opposed to National Pork Council's facts that show when folks are not choosing red meat they are choosing chicken for dinner.

You can have fun with your slogan, but true brand positioning identifies the brand, its category, and its relevance to your target audience, and speaks to the brand's relativity to the competition. Like I said before, it's a big, crowded, crazy-competitive world out there and a good focused position can deliver a brand win.

Brand Messaging

Next on the list after defining your brand position is creating your brand message and understanding the difference between your company's brand message and its mission statement. Whereas your mission statement is a formal summary of the aims and values of your company and meant as an internal compass for your employees, your brand message is the external conveyance of the value proposition that you establish. It's important to remember that your mission statement should be included in your brand message, but your brand message shouldn't necessarily be included in your mission statement.

In addition, it's also of the utmost importance that you remember the following fact as you develop your brand message: consumers build brands. Consumers develop particular expectations when they engage with your brand, and it's your goal to help their experiences achieve your brand promise. Remember that your company is ultimately a storyteller, and consumers will buy into your story and develop an affinity with your brand if it resonates.

My own experiences and general industry knowledge suggests an effective brand message includes three important elements: the development of a value proposition, the development of a brand promise, and the development of a brand position and brand-positioning statement. Each of these elements is an integral part of your brand message foundation. Before I discuss brand positioning, which forms the very core of your brand message, I'll first address brand promise as well as its value proposition.

Value Proposition

A value proposition is a statement that clearly identifies measurable and demonstrable benefits your customers receive when they are buying your product. Your value proposition essentially represents the factual basis of your brand promise by specifically stating what differentiates your product from others. It should convince employees, stakeholders, and consumers that your product is better than the others on the market, based on an analysis of costs and benefits with the value equaling the benefits minus the costs. A powerful value proposition gives your company direction, creates focus, breeds internal confidence, and improves customer understanding and engagement.

Brand Promise

A brand promise represents the value or experience a company's customer can expect to receive each time they interact with that company and its products. If the company can deliver a positive experience on a consistent basis, their brand affinity and value will increase in the minds of both consumers and employees. Your brand becomes something special. In my experience, a powerful brand promise possesses the following attributes:

Simple and memorable. Your brand promise should be no longer than a simple sentence or two, and it must be memorable enough for employees to embrace it and feel like they want to use it during customer interactions.

Genuine and sincere. Your brand promise should be more than just a catchy phrase or a punchy slogan. It must be authentic and tangible. If the customer experience doesn't match the brand promise, the value of your brand is weakened.

Different. Your brand promise should represent the very essence of your company and convey what makes your company and its products truly unique.

Inspiring. Your brand promise should cultivate a positive emotional connection between consumers and your products. It should be thoughtful and relevant without becoming a promise you cannot deliver.

Coca-Cola and Brand Messaging

While it may seem to be a very different type of company than yours, beverage giant Coca-Cola can serve as a familiar example of the intricacies of brand messaging. Granted, it has evolved over the years, but Coca Cola's message clarifies that it knows where it stands and how it wants to be viewed. Here is a general breakdown of the company's brand message structure, which I cobbled together from several industry sources:

Brand Message: Taste the Feeling.

Brand Promise: Coca-Cola inspires moments of optimism and cheer.

Value proposition: Coca-Cola offers everyone a unique experience of happiness (at a relatively low cost).

Brand position: Coca-Cola is the cola of the world.

Employees and Brand Messaging

While it's important to emphasize brand position for your consumers, you cannot neglect employment branding. Employment branding is the perception that past, current, and prospective future employees have about their experience with a company. Cultivating a brand that connects and resonates with employees is just as important as cultivating a brand that does so with consumers. Consumers still build brands, but past, present, and future employees can help mold that building process. The values and the mission of your company should be thoroughly present in its daily operation.

More Brand Advantage Strategies: An Overview

Having nailed down your brand message as well as your brand position, I'll address several other brand advantage strategies within the upcoming chapters in this section. These strategies include the establishment of your branded visual voice, the development of specific brand packaging, and the creation of branded campaign elements.

I would argue that your branded visual voice is sometimes even more important than the words you use during the creation of your brand message. Chapter 8 discusses your brand's visual identity and how to employ your identity with logos, branded programs, point-of-purchase marketing, and shopper marketing. I'll also discuss business-to-business sale support materials, which will help you expose your brand and brand programs to your buyers and retailers. Furthermore, I'll then address the finer details of visual layout and packaging style, including style guides, font options, color schemes, and the use of photographs and other visual materials.

In Chapter 9, I'll turn to product packaging, which is a very important factor to get right because you must communicate a lot in a very short period of time. Like a point-of-purchase product ad or billboard, your packaging must excel in the most competitive of environments. In short, your packaging must stand out, be simple, and, if possible, trigger an emotional response that leaves a lasting impression—all in a matter of seconds. How price point and perceived value factor into the packaging mix, among other things, will also be discussed.

Chapter 10 focuses on your branded campaign elements, which begins with what is called a messaging matrix. Basically, a messaging matrix is a simple visual model used to determine what a branded campaign message is about and if it will resonate with your core target audience. Your brand cannot mean everything to everyone, but it can offer something for a wider audience than just your core. Chapter 10 also addresses traditional marketing outlets for your brand, including advertisements, free-standing inserts, billboards, radio, newspapers, and television, as well as digital outlets such as websites and social media.

Chapter 8

BRANDED VISUAL IDENTITY

It's always comforting to see a familiar and friendly face. I love the way my dog reacts when I walk in the door every evening—so happy and bouncy. The feeling is reciprocal. I see her, and I can't help but smile. I have similar feelings when I see my Fender Telecaster guitar or my college mascot, the Kansas Jayhawk. I have so many great feelings and memories tied to those brand images. I've seen a similar look on people's travel-weary faces when they see a Starbucks in an airport. That color palette, the fonts, and the logo all act as powerful visual cues: Our old friend Starbucks is here.

Starbucks is just one among hundreds of companies that masterfully use their visual branding to not only stand out in a crowded, cluttered, and competitive market, but also to act as a visual cue that says a familiar friend in a trusted brand is nearby.

In business, when someone develops an affinity with your brand's identity, they like the comfort of knowing that they can quickly recognize you in the crowd. I've said it before, and I'll say it again—ours is an over communicated world, one oversaturated with messaging. Treat your fan base well and make life easier. After all, your audience's experience is much more important than your boredom with the same identity. Remember, it's not about you—it's about your audience.

Branding is about simplicity, commitment, perseverance, patience, and being "sticky". When you do the due diligence and really identify who you are in the marketplace versus how you can differentiate yourself and your brand, you should commit to it, build on it, and stay the course. No brand is built overnight.

This chapter will address the various aspects of developing a powerful visual language for your brand. Our discussion will begin with the firm establishment of your brand identity and continue through logos and branded programs, packaging, style guides, and sales support materials.

BRANDED VISUAL IDENTITY

Insofar as your brand is your company's corporate image and encompasses its overall values and aims—everything it does, owns, and produces—your brand's visual identity is the outward expression of that brand. This outward expression should convey all the attributes, values, purposes, strengths, and passions of your brand. As opposed to your brand image, which is the consumer's perception of your brand, your brand identity is a representation of how your company wants to be perceived.

A brand's visual identity consists of several obvious factors including a logo, but it also includes other visual aspects of a brand such as color schemes, typography, and fonts. Whereas a brand is the unique combination of words, messaging, images, and symbols used to differentiate a product or organization from the competition, a brand's visual identity is all the visual components of that brand. Together, they define the brand within all company communications.

The branded visual identity of a company is comprised of anything and everything visual that represents the business, including the following:

Logo: The mark or symbol that identifies a brand and/or an organization.

Stationery: Letterhead, envelopes, business cards, etc.

Marketing Collateral: Fliers, brochures, books, websites, etc.

Products and Packaging: What a company sells and what it comes in.

Message and Actions: Everything conveyed within internal and external communications.

Apparel Design: Clothing worn by employees and distributed to the public.

Signage: Interior and exterior design.

A brand is one of the most valuable assets of any business, and it needs to be crafted carefully so that it is unique and memorable while also effectively differentiating a company's products within the marketplace.

The Brand Identity Prism

Here's a little history lesson on brand identity. The term *brand identity* was first mentioned by corporate branding specialist Jean-Noel Kapferer in 1986. He developed what came to be called the brand identity prism, which can be visualized as a six-sided prism that identifies all the different but interrelated aspects of brand identity as Kapferer sees them. They include physique, personality, culture, relationship, reflection, and self-image, which are defined as follows:

Physique: The physical aspect of the brand, including the company's logo, color scheme, packaging, and online presence.

Personality: The brand's character as it is communicated to the outside world, including writing tone and style, design style, and color scheme.

Culture: The value system and basic principles upon which a brand bases its behavior.

Relationship: The relationship between potential consumers that a brand wishes to symbolize. For example, the relationships among friends or between parents and their children.

Reflection: What a company sees as its most stereotypical customer.

Self-Image: How a company's stereotypical customer sees themselves.

Within the prism, these six aspects are interlocked in relationships that enable companies to see themselves both as their own "selves" and as the customer. At NewPoint, we call this process "brand foundation" and find many aspects of the prism concept applicable to the identities of food brands we work with today.

Establishing Your Visual Identity

With a good product and consistent use, developing your brand identity—one that resonates with a specific demographic—can generate loyalty and repeat customers. Remember that simplicity and commitment are the cornerstones of an identity that forms the foundation for a fan base. The human mind is interesting, considering it interprets visual images as very powerful and concise messages, and there are numerous images out there to interpret.

The internet has vastly increased the amount of visualized information available to users. Almost half of our brains are involved in visual processing, and 70 percent of all our sensory receptors are in our eyes. We can take in a visual scene in less than one-tenth of a second. Being able to maintain consistency and differentiation for your brand is, therefore, of the utmost importance, especially for loyal customers.

Specifically, a brand's visual identity is composed of color palettes, typography, composition, and photographs. These components make it easy for customers to identify your brand in a crowded marketplace. According to a CBS News report, the average American sees as many as 5,000 unique ads a day. That's a lot of different brand messages attempting to break through the marketing clutter—and your message may be number 5,001. There are advantages to having a brand identity that transcends all media so consumers who encounter your brand are easily able to recognize your company no matter when, where, or how they might encounter it.

Essentially, your visual identity is the sum of all the parts mentioned previously. Each component plays a role, and if your visuals are not consistent across all media, then your story is not whole. The process of establishing your branded visual identity begins with identifying your target audience and continues through your brand story, your brand personality, and your brand's emotional appeal. Many of these things were covered in the previous chapter, but what you must do here is envision how you will translate those foundational concepts into proper visual representations.

Who Is Your Target Audience?

Understanding both the demographics and the psychographics of your target audience cannot be stressed enough. It's important to tailor your message, of course, but ensuring that you're speaking with the right people is also critical. Creating a buyer persona—an ideal customer—will strengthen your messaging because you'll know exactly what type of person you will be addressing.

Target audience discovery will be discussed in detail in later chapters, but it boils down to a few basic ideas:

The 80/20 Rule. This is a time-tested rule in business and marketing, which states that 80 percent of your product sales will be bought by just 20 percent of the shopping public. It's up to you to identify that 20 percent and focus your efforts on them.

The mom Rule. In America today, mom is truly the matriarch when it comes to making the food-buying decisions. Always keep her in mind while you make your marketing decisions.

The Millennial Rule. Millennials are a large and ever-growing portion of consumers, and their shopping behavior and product preferences hold an increasing amount of sway in today's evolving food industry marketplace. Get dialed in to the millennial mind-set because its importance is only going to grow in the future.

Who Are You?

Reflecting on your mission statement and the various aspects of your branded message is a good start here. Your brand is a story, and if your story resonates with your audience, they'll be interested in what else you should say. Giving them that reason to look for you in the market landscape will be crucial for your growth. Loyal customers effectively promote your brand to their friends. And word of mouth, fueled by a compelling story that is backed by powerful visuals, is incredibly valuable.

What Is Your Brand's Personality?

Aristotle defined three modes of persuasion: logos, ethos, and pathos. Logos and ethos appeal to logic and credibility, respectively, while pathos appeals to emotion. What is your brand's emotional appeal? How does your audience rationalize your message? Infusing your message with emotion reinforces your brand personality and fosters a bond between your brand and your fan base, therefore, cultivating a lasting perception.

When it comes to brand personality, you should ask yourself a few fundamental questions. What does your brand look and sound like? Is it refined, eccentric, quirky, or authentic? What visual design style, including color schemes and font types, matches it? Understanding your brand personality is just as important as understanding who your target audience is.

LOGOS AND BRANDED PROGRAMS

Now that you have poured the foundations of your branded visual identity, it's time to begin building up the house—logo, color palette, typography, and photography. Your brand identity will be seen in both traditional and digital advertisements, of course. More importantly, however, is the fact that it will be seen quite often on your brand packaging. Therefore, that's where to begin.

Logo

A brand logo, as defined by the American Marketing Association, is a graphic design that is used as a continuing symbol for a company, organization, or brand. Typically, a logo can be a mark, flag, symbol, or signature that is designed for use across various media. The attributes of an effective logo are much like the aspects of a powerful brand promise. They are ...

Unique to your brand. Your logo should be easily identifiable against the competition.

Simple and memorable. Your logo should be easily recognizable. Also, if it's simple, then it's easily remembered. Think of the logo for General Mills or Apple. Both are minimalist, but still possess strong recognition with consumers. The challenge is that a logo should feature unique characteristics without being overly flashy.

Adaptable. A logo should work in every medium and application. To elaborate, will this logo be effective if it's printed in a single color, or if it's as small as a postage stamp or as large as a billboard?

Relevant. Is your logo consistent with your brand? Should you use ˑ silly colors, and fonts? Or, should it be more serious and clean cut? ˑ a logo consistent with your company aids in the brand messag- ˑmers and employees.

Sustainable. It's helpful to design a logo that can endure for years or even decades. If your company ever expands, there's a good chance your logo will need to evolve. For example, Coca-Cola has retained its logo for almost a century and a half. Meanwhile, Pepsi has undergone frequent logo changes and iterations. The creation of a timeless logo encourages a nostalgic connection with long-time users and is therefore priceless.

Positioning your logo and determining how much room to leave in the area surrounding it may seem trivial, but a logo's importance illustrates the exactitude and consistency needed during the creation of your brand's visual identity. Positioning and spacing are important guidelines to have written out so that designers know exactly how creative they can get, both initially and during brand development.

Color Palette

Your chosen color palette must truly breathe the personality of your brand. It accentuates and cements the perception that your audience has of your brand. Your choice of colors is also important because, according to a 2016 entrepreneur.com article, a study called "The Impact of Color in Marketing" found that up to 90 percent of snap judgments made about products can be based on color alone. Although individual consumer responses to different colors is dependent on their personal experiences, we have found that there are some general guidelines, including the following:

Yellow: Projects optimism, warmth, and clarity.
Orange: Projects friendliness, cheerfulness, and confidence.
Red: Projects excitement, youthfulness, and boldness.
Blue: Projects trust, dependability, and strength.

Typography and Font Choices

The typography and fonts you choose are just as important as your chosen color palette because they're all building blocks for your brand personality. Typefaces and fonts not only help determine how eloquent-looking and legible your copy and other content will be, they also possess a personality and a voice. That's why I believe choosing the right typefaces and fonts for your brand is so—because it's an essential way to convey your brand message to your target audience. For example, you probably wouldn't want to use a bold strong font (like **STENCIL**) if your product was baby food, and you wouldn't want a playful font (like *Euphoria Script*) if your product was beef jerky. Often, you will choose to feature several different typefaces and fonts, with each one addressing different messages that can change, depending on the mood that the brand wants to employ.

Style Guides

Style guides are necessary when consistency is critical to brand recognition. Think of your style guide as your company's bible when it comes to branded visuals, voice, and messaging. Having an acceptable guide helps when you want to scale your marketing. You won't have to spend time conveying to designers how you want the logo placed, which fonts to use, or what color palettes they should or shouldn't use. Your style guide is a timesaver and an investment for scaling your company when the time comes. Style guides are also useful when it comes to internal memos, press releases, package designs, websites, advertisements, and inserts.

Photography and Video

Good photography can provoke powerful emotions and food photography is no different. Instagram is filled with big and small brands that are doing some great work building and connecting with their core audience through branded photography. We cannot stress enough the importance of maintaining a substantial photo budget in your annual marketing plan so that you can partner with an art director who understands your brand requirements and a food photographer with a full studio.

Buzzfeed's Tasty food videos have fed the desire of foodies to learn new recipes, and these videos are a huge contributing factor in the explosion in popularity of branded food videos proliferating on all social media feeds from YouTube and Facebook to Instagram and Snapchat. Much depends on you presenting a good visual for your brand. Cultivate and hire great talent to produce your food videos.

Packaging

When shoppers are at the store looking at products, they're not necessarily making rational decisions. According to a 2016 *Journal of Applied Packaging Research* study, which is discussed at length in Chapter 9, consumers spend only about three to five seconds examining products on the shelves before purchase. This study also found that, even though consumers have generally decided beforehand what kinds of products they want, 28 percent of them make their final decision—brand selection—in the store. Furthermore, the study indicated that 1 out of 10 purchasers may change their brand preference inside the store. Instead of thinking their way to the checkout, consumer purchases tend to be instinctive and reactive. They are purchasing instinctively by color, shape, and familiarity of location.

Effective packaging should encompass the entirety of your brand identity so that consumers can see at a glance what the product is and why it's relevant to them. The product must deliver its brand promise each time, which fosters repeat purchases and encourages brand loyalty. Packaging will be covered in the next chapter.

Point-of-Purchase Displays and Shopper Marketing

How will you be positioning your product in a retail market? How are you going to differentiate it among the hundreds of products lining the shelves? One marketing tool is point-of-purchase (POP). POP is commonly found in aisles, on shelves, and at the checkout—anywhere a consumer makes a decision about whether to put your product in their cart. These can be as simple as dividers in the meat cooler or as complex as elaborate mid-aisle displays.

Point-of-purchase displays are just one facet of the increasing emphasis on shopper marketing. Shopper marketing is an attempt to appeal to customers at the exact moment they are prepared to buy something. Unlike other media buys, where the goal is to linger in the minds of customers, shopper marketing tries to make an immediate impact and directly influence behavior.

This kind of in-the-moment of decision appeals to consumers takes many forms. Grocery stores have long offered free samples, hoping to whet a customer's appetite when it's easiest for them to buy food. Beer and chip makers construct elaborate promotional displays in store aisles at the start of each football season. High-end stores even use careful calibrations of light, space, music, and ambiance to put customers in the mood to shop. Some of the most fundamental shopper marketing techniques include on-shelf or on-package coupons to invite trial, personal check-out coupons, floor graphics, cart/basket advertising, and shelf signs.

Sales Support Materials

With a style guide in place, you can create sales support materials. These materials are crucial for any company that operates in the retail arena and encompass the entirety of your outward-facing identity. Your support materials should comprise of some of or all the following items:

* A comprehensive marketing program, which consists of the following:
    * All digital content regarding the product, including websites, online ads, blogs, boosted social media posts, loyalty clubs, email marketing, digital coupons, and retailer card offers.
    * All traditional marketing plans, including television ads, radio ads, newspaper ads, magazine ads, and free-standing inserts (FSIs).
* Product data sheets that contain the product's detailed specifications.
* Sales brochures and other printed product information that encompasses your whole product portfolio.
* Visual aids used in sales presentations, including videos and animation.

One good way to measure the effectiveness of your sales support materials and your visual brand in general is to look at them from an outsider's perspective. It's important that your materials are both unique and informative. If you, acting as an outsider, aren't moved by your sales support materials, then real shoppers probably won't be either. To that end, ask yourself these questions:

* Does the message and visuals match up or tell the brand's story?
* Is there something about this that is compelling and unique from my competition?
* Is it easy to find the answers to the important questions—the ones that will help in the decision-making process?
* Finally, and most importantly, are my sales support materials convincing?

CONCLUSION

Know yourself and know your audience. Remain committed and persevere. Keep it simple, be consistent, and plan for change. And, finally, stand out from the crowd. These are mantras you should live by as you develop your brand's identity and its multifaceted visual voice. In the end, this is how the other players in your world, from your competitors to your consumers, will see you.

Chapter 9

PACKAGING

How great would it be if your brand was instantly recognizable to almost 100 percent of your target market? Well, Coca-Cola is exactly that, and Coca-Cola's target market is everyone on Earth.

It's common knowledge in the business and marketing worlds that Coca-Cola's logo is recognizable to a whopping 94 percent of the world's population, but what many of those millions truly recognize is more than the logo. It's Coca-Cola's whole package. The vibrant red-and-white contrast of its color scheme. The rakish style of its typeface. The dynamic contours of its original container—that iconic fluted glass bottle, which still appears as an image on Coca-Cola packages today. That's first-class packaging at work, and it's turned Coca-Cola into one of the biggest fish in the food industry pond.

Now it's your turn. You understand your place in the evolving market. You've studied the demographics and psychographics, so you're familiar with the tastes and preferences of your target market. You know the competition and you know your planograms. From your mission, message, position, and identity to your colors, fonts, and styles, you know it all. Now for the hard part: convincing end-line consumers to choose your product over all the others in a matter of seconds.

In many ways, your brand's packaging is just as important as the product it contains. By definition, product packaging simply consists of all aspects of the container that a product comes in, including materials, shape, graphics, and additional features such as openings, closures, caps, and dispensers. However, your brand's packaging means much more than that. Done right, your packaging will attract shoppers, make your brand stand out, facilitate purchase, tell your story, and encourage brand loyalty, all in the blink of an eye in the most competitive of environments.

When you consider all of this, designing your brand packaging offers a great opportunity to outshine the competition based on the following facts:

* According to a study by the Journal of Applied Packaging Research, consumers spend approximately two to three seconds examining a product on the shelves and a full 90 percent of consumers make a buying decision based on the packaging alone.
* According to a study by the shopping analysis company WestRock, approximately 66 percent of consumers tried something new because the packaging caught their eye and 35 percent of consumers changed brands because of new packaging.
* According to numerous sources, an estimated 70 percent of all purchasing decisions are made at the retail shelf.

It's obvious that your packaging design is a critical factor for your company's survival and growth. In addition, there's a lot of information that needs to be conveyed very fast in a world that's already very overstimulated.

Relying heavily on my own extensive experience as well as exhaustive recent market reports by WestRock and the *Journal of Applied Packaging Research* as well as other industry research, I'll use this chapter to discuss all the facets of effective packaging in detail. I'll begin with the business-to-customer side of your packaging, including its role as a brand ambassador and difference-maker, as well as the fundamentals of nutrition labeling and the rise of clean labeling. I'll also address the more practical areas of packaging such as functionality and safety. Together, the aesthetic and functional attributes of your packaging can make the difference between success and failure for you, your company, and its brand.

THE WHOLE PACKAGE ON PACKAGING
Packaging Basics

For the purposes of marketing, packaging consists of logos, labels, nutritional information, color and design schemes, and the packaging materials themselves. The basic functions of product packaging are to protect the product from damage, attract consumers to the product, promote the product and the overall brand, facilitate purchase, and differentiate one branded product from another. The goal of product packaging is to initiate a relationship with consumers, encourage familiarity through repeated purchase, and build brand loyalty.

There are several things packaging must do well to be successful. To help communicate this, I often refer to a *Forbes* report, which states that effective product packaging must stand out, be simple, pass the five-year-old test, trigger emotional engagement, and create iconic assets. You can accomplish these as follows:

* **Stand out.** Use the shape, size, color, and logo orientation to draw the eyes of shoppers and communicate the essence of the proposition.
* **Be simple.** Clarity and good use of white space can make a product stand out in a visually agitated and busy market.
* **Pass the five-year-old test.** Determine if a five-year-old can find and identify a specific branded product when they are armed with nothing more than a brief description of the packaging.

* **Trigger emotional engagement.** Create moments of meaningful feelings for consumers, often through design, photographs, or other compelling imagery that encourages eye contact.
* **Create iconic assets.** Create a series of visual equities that trigger lasting memories, such as the combination of popping color contrasts, stylish cursive typeface, and dynamically contoured shapes found in Coca-Cola's packaging.

This must-do list begins with the initial act of recognition and purchase through differentiation. The numbers don't lie—consumers act instinctively and almost instantaneously based on packaging alone. While there are other aspects of product packaging that influence consumer behavior, several of which will be discussed here, it all begins with these packaging basics.

Packaging and Food Safety

There's perhaps nothing that's more important to your company, your buyers/retailers, and the end-line consumer than food safety. Food safety begins with you (production), continues through your retailers and buyers (distribution), and ends with your consumers (consumption). Ensuring food safety isn't important simply because it helps you avoid public relations disaster. It's also of the utmost importance to consumer trust, and safe product packaging is the best way to gain trust on the consumer end.

The WestRock study produced the following results regarding the building of consumer trust in brands:

* More than 75 percent of consumers said it would be extremely or very impactful to their trust in a brand to "package products in ways that protect them from tampering and contamination".

* Seventy-seven percent of consumers consider packaging that protects them from tampering and contamination as the most impactful operation activity manufacturers can engage in to gain consumer trust regarding product safety. This percentage is higher than that for high-quality ingredients, honest labeling, safe packaging materials, and safe design.
* More than 80 percent of consumers say safe packaging makes them more favorable toward a manufacturer or brand (88 percent), trust the brand more (80 percent), and more likely to recommend products from the manufacturer or brand to friends and family (82 percent).

Furthermore, while WestRock found that 92 percent of consumers believed that packaging safety is headed in the right direction, 25 percent of them said brands are not doing enough to ensure that packaging doesn't contain harmful materials or substances. There's clearly room for improvement when it comes to the perception of packaging safety, which translates into an opportunity for you and your company to differentiate your product in the eyes of your buyers and consumers.

Packaging and Labels

Most packaging in the food industry includes labeling information printed on the package that's intended to assist the customer in their product choices. Shoppers rely on food labels to tell them what a product contains, its nutritional value, and how it was produced. In fact, according to WestRock, 70 percent of consumers used packaging to learn more about products. Food producers rely on labels to capture the attention of shoppers and encourage purchase through the promotion of the desirable attributes of their products, such as health benefits and sustainability.

There are several aspects of food product labeling that must be addressed. They include the legal requirements regarding nutritional information, the increasing consumer desire for sustainable products and "clean" labeling, as well as the muddy waters of consumer perceptions regarding labeling practices and regulations.

Nutrition Facts Label Changes

In 2016, the Food and Drug Association presented a new Nutrition Facts label for packaged foods. This new label, which hadn't been updated in more than 20 years, is designed to reflect new scientific information that recognizes the link between obesity and heart disease and makes it easier for consumers to make more informed food choices in general. Manufacturers with more than $10 million in annual food sales must comply with the new Nutrition Facts label regulations by July 26, 2018, while manufacturers who make less than $10 million have until July 2019 to comply.

The complete FDA report and its findings can be found in the Guidance and Regulations section on the FDA website (www.fda.gov), but here are a few of its important highlights:

Refreshed design. Increases the size of the print presence of the calorie count, serving size, and servings per container listings; requires the declaration of the actual amounts of certain vitamins and minerals; better explains the meaning of Percent Daily Value in the footnote.

Updated nutrition information. Includes added sugars in grams and as Percent Daily Value; updates the list of nutrients that are required or permitted to be declared; removes fat calories from a required list that still includes total fat, saturated fat, and trans fat; updates daily values for nutrients such as sodium, dietary fiber, and vitamin D.

Updated serving size requirements. Follows the law by stating that serving sizes must be based on amounts of foods and beverages people are eating, not what they should be eating. To that end, some smaller packages will be required to be listed as one serving only and some larger packages will be required to list both per-serving and per-package listings on their labels.

Labels and Consumer Confusion

The fact is that what appears on much food packaging is only loosely regulated, difficult to verify, frequently misleading, and sometimes downright deceptive. This can often lead to consumer confusion and distrust. Consumer confusion is something that a truly savvy company will take advantage of, not by deceiving its consumers with a scheme that carries the potential for long-term disaster, but by using nutrition labeling as an opportunity to build brand affinity with the confused consumer.

A study by two McGill University psychologists found that standard U.S. food package labels rate as the worst amongst the four differing nutrition-labeling schemes that it studied, leading consumers to the least nutritious food-buying decisions. In fact, the Nutrition Facts label on U.S. packages wasn't only less helpful than the other labels studied, it also required more time to review and understand than the others. All of this led my NewPoint team to create the following list of key concepts to keep in mind while you consider nutrition labeling:

Assume your consumers know nothing. Don't take anything for granted when it comes to the knowledge or perceptions of your consumers.

Educate your consumers. Introducing a new concept, such as an updated nutrition label, will likely require consumer education. Remember that these are uninitiated consumers with which you are dealing.

Give your consumers a scale. Your consumers will need a starting point from which to begin judging the claims your label is making. For example, if your product claims to be low-carb, provide an example of a product that isn't as low-carb when compared to yours.

Create a brand-wide scale. If it applies, consider employing one product's scaling model throughout all the products in your brand to provide consistency and encourage brand affinity.

A simple action such as making subtle changes to a seemingly trivial thing like your nutrition labels can help you turn a confused consumer into a loyal one. Providing consumers with a useful tool to make better buying decisions for themselves and their families can go a long way to building valuable brand trust and delivering on the higher brand expectations of consumers.

Clean Labeling

The rise of what industry insiders and consumers alike call "clean" labeling is something for a local, small, or regional company on the move to investigate. According to foodbusiness.net, which conducted several related studies regarding the clean label movement, perhaps the simplest way to look at this movement is to consider it a desire for clear and concise declarations of ingredients. For the most part, what consumers want are ingredient lists they understand and lists that are filled with things that are, in their minds, less processed.

The clean label movement is, in many ways, part of the more general increase in consumer preferences for healthier foods and transparency on the part of manufacturers that is driving the evolving food marketplace. The foodbusiness.net research indicates that many industry insiders believe that the clean label movement is more sustainable than a mere trend. While the core followers of clean eating represented only 5 percent of primary grocery shoppers as of 2015, the fact that 80 percent of clean eaters consider clean eating a lifestyle rather than a diet or fad may give the movement more staying power. Additionally, more than 50 percent of clean eaters have been practicing the lifestyle for more than a year, which suggests both staying power and future growth.

According to these same studies, the clean eating lifestyle is also attractive to consumers of all ages. Healthy eating and manufacturer transparency are hallmark traits of the increasingly influential millennial generation, of course, and its preference for clean labeling comes as no surprise. In addition, many older people are also attracted to the lifestyle due to concerns about overall health more than because of their preference for natural products. This demographic also tends to have the money to spend on clean label products.

Clean labeling does have its potential pitfalls. Consumer confusion and the potential for perceived deception on the manufacturers' part are real issues as we discussed previously, and clean labeling runs the risk of falling into those treacherous waters. Many food and beverage companies have already started using such terms as *clean, artisan, earth-friendly, local, pure,* and *simple* as product descriptors, all of which might soon join *natural* on the consumers' list of products promises that are under scrutiny.

Companies interested in switching to clean labeling must also consider the facts that developing clean products isn't simple. Developing clean label products can be expensive, and it can be difficult to align clean labeling with other consumer health trends. Furthermore, some products are unfit to make clean label claims by nature, and products with simpler ingredients also may have a shorter shelf life.

Packaging and Sustainability

Within this chapter's discussion about packaging, I've generally divided the topic into two categories: the marketing side and the functional side. In many ways, however, sustainability as a factor in your packaging decisions falls into both categories because it involves both consumer preferences for partnering with socially conscious and environmentally friendly businesses and the physical nature of the packaging itself. The packaging serves as both a label and a vessel. Satisfying consumers on both fronts requires a deft balancing act.

While *sustainability* is like several other food industry terms in that it does not yet have a legal definition, sustainweb.org came up with a suitable working definition. According to this website, sustainable food should be produced, processed, distributed, and disposed of in ways that:

* Contribute to thriving local economies and sustainable livelihoods.
* Protect the diversity of both plants and animals.
* Avoid damaging or wasting natural resources or contributing to climate change.
* Provide social benefits, such as high-quality food, safe and healthy products, and educational opportunities.

When it comes to how consumers view brands, sustainability is a crucial factor. According to the WestRock report, a whopping 98 percent of consumers surveyed indicated that sustainability is either extremely or very important to their view of a brand.

Alignment with consumer preferences for dealing with companies that make sustainable products can be done in several ways from public communications, such as company websites, speeches, and promotions to the use of renewable energy during production and distribution. According to WestRock, however, the packaging itself is by far the best way for a company to demonstrate its commitment to sustainability.

Packaging is where the balancing act comes into play: consumers want packaging to be efficient and eco-friendly, but they also want it to satisfy their desire for increased freshness, ease of use, and minimal damage in the products they are purchasing. WestRock reports that 78 percent of consumers believe it's most important for brands to focus on innovations that make their products easier to use, while 77 percent say it is extremely/very important for that packaging to keep products fresh and 82 percent say it is extremely/very important that packaging prevent spilling or breaking. Also, as mentioned previously, consumers are very concerned about packaging safety.

Well, which is it—personal philosophy or functionality? Are consumers buying with their minds, or are they buying with their stomachs? Actually, consumers want both. The simplest solution to this broad and complex issue is for a company to choose a good and economical packaging fit for their products from the existing pool of materials that have been deemed sustainable.

A Case Study: Purely Fake Honey

The *Journal of Applied Packaging Research* conducted a complex case study that explored the benefits of a consumer-based approach to food packaging design. Using a fictitious honey brand called "Melitimo," which loosely means "precious honey" in Greek, the research company studied the impact of packaging in the development of product identity and the resulting perceived meaning for consumers. Here's a collection of some of the study's general findings on packaging impact:

* The package is the product, particularly for low-involvement products such as foods and beverages where initial impressions at the point of sale can have a lasting impact.

* Packaging that is congruent with a product's attributes can help form more appropriate consumer expectations, and therefore, potentially enhance the consumption experience.
* The size and shape of a product's packaging greatly affects the decision-making process. Consumers tend to make simplified judgments regarding product volume and value, giving longer or larger packaging generally increased perceived value, and thus, resulting in better sales.
* Labeling has become a crucial ambassador for products as healthy eating has increased in popularity, but detailed product information is not as important in low-involvement products.
* Packaging technology and the convenience it implies may be the most important attribute when it comes to consumers' prospects to buy.

The study had more specific findings when it came to Melitimo. The honey study presented survey participants with a variety of packaging options, including visual categories such as graphics and size/shape as well as information elements that consisted of product details and technology applied on the package. The survey parameter that the study's authors found most fundamental in their proposed packaging concept creation came at the survey's conclusion. At that point, they simply asked consumers, "Which of these 10 Melitimo Honey products would you purchase?" Following are descriptions of the top three selected concepts, all of which featured a gold color scheme with other earthy tones:

* A concept that was basically a package functioning as the object itself—a beehive—and was playful, inviting users to participate in its use in a more vibrant way.

* A concept that featured a classic wide-mouthed glass jar, which conveyed a nostalgic fascination of a bygone era through sterile typography and a refined homage to beauty and timelessness.
* A concept that took the hexagonal shape of a honeycomb and featured a simple message, suggesting innovation, minimalism, and modernism.

The study's conclusion supported existing scholarship that states, "packaging that contains a distinct shape, color, orientation, contrast, or size will attract consumers' visual attention and influence peoples' reaction and buying behavior regardless of their specific brand preferences." The complete study and all its findings can be found at http://scholarworks.rit.edu.

A Case Study: Packaging and Big Beer

Whether it's time to tailgate, cook out, lounge on the beach, do yard work, or go golfing, it seems like it's always time for a beer. Add that to the generally accepted rule of thumb that roughly 80 percent of beer sold in America will be bought by just 20 percent of consumers, one would think that beer brands shouldn't have to work that hard to sell their products. Yet, work hard they do because they want to grow, and they know that a large percentage (40+) of the market is not fully brand loyal.

It comes as no surprise then that even big beer companies have incentive to capture and keep the market's attention. However, because beer brand loyalty is largely based on taste, the bigger brands don't want to mess with that (a margarita-flavored Tequiza, anyone?). Instead, they seek continued market interest through new and innovative packaging designs. Packaging innovation drives consumer trial.

Some of the more popular innovations beer companies have implemented in recent years include frost brew can lining, two-stage cold activation, wide-mouth cans, and punch-top cans. One of the best recent packaging innovations, in our opinion, is the CO_2 ball that Guinness introduced to its canned products so that its beer tastes like it came right from the tap—brilliant!

In addition, there are also countless packaging innovations that will come and go (and for good reason), such as Budweiser's bow tie-shaped can and Miller Lite's vortex bottle. Then again, Miller recently got one thing right in terms of packaging when it introduced a retro-style Miller Lite packaging scheme. By doing nothing more than tweaking the packaging, Miller Lite sales jumped nearly five percent. The point here is this: even heavy hitters in the food and beverage industry feel the need to maintain the attention of their target audience through new and innovative packaging designs.

Packaging and Your Buyer/Retailer

While your goal is to sell your product to the end-line consumer, your first hurdle is being able to sell it to your buyers, retailers, and category managers. Both the marketing side of your packaging design and the functional side of it are of the utmost importance during these interactions. Buyers and retailers love experts, as I've said before, and this is where you prove that you *are* one. They want to see that you know who you want to sell to and how you want to sell it, while also understanding the importance of freshness, safety, and the durability required of your packaging during the distribution process. Your interactions with buyers and retailers provide you with your first opportunity to show that you can go for the kill and really sell your product, first to them and then to the consumer. Details on buyer/retailer enticement will be discussed in the next chapter.

CONCLUSION

You work very hard on making your products and for good reason, but it's quite possible that your product's packaging is just as important as the product itself. Your packaging represents the point of your company's spear as it serves as its first impression, differentiator, and brand ambassador, and must instantly strike deep into the hearts and minds of your consumers. Your packaging is the bait that lures consumers, and every consumer lured represents another step you have made up the food chain.

Chapter 10

BRANDED CAMPAIGNS

Your company and its brand now have a well-defined mission, a carefully honed message, and a compelling visual identity. You know your position in the marketplace. Now it's time to get to work on consumer awareness of your brand, which is where your marketing campaigns come into play.

By definition, a marketing campaign is a specific and defined series of activities used in marketing a new or changed product or a series of activities launched in new marketing channels and methods. These channels include various digital marketing channels and social media, as well as traditional marketing channels such as print and broadcast media. While your company's mission, message, and visual identity are likely to remain relatively constant over time, lasting up to a decade or longer, the marketing campaigns you develop should less permanent. Your campaigns should be considered as annual or even seasonal methods of establishing, maintaining, and increasing consumer brand awareness.

For you, campaigns are an opportunity to deliver the essence of your brand message to consumers using different hooks that appeal to their behaviors and preferences at specific moments in time. Campaigns function as ways to invite consumer trial, unveil product innovations, promote deals, and highlight seasonal relevance. And, while marketing campaigns might come and go, they should always be carefully researched, well-executed, time-sensitive, and goal-oriented. At the end of the day, effective campaigns are often what separates growing companies from those with stagnant sales and no growth. Plus, as we heard from buyers in Chapter 3, they want you to help drive your products towards sales. Effective campaigns do that.

In this chapter, I'll address both digital and traditional media marketing campaign channels. The advantages and disadvantages of these channels will be discussed, as well as how to map out a method for evaluating effective marketing campaigns. Additionally, I'll also address the measurement and analysis of campaigns, as well as the roles that retailers and buyers play within the campaign structure.

DIGITAL MEDIA MARKETING CHANNELS

Digital media marketing channels basically include everything that is available online. As the times continue to change, email and social media campaigns are taking the place of direct mail campaigns. Internet campaigns generally perform similar functions as both newspapers and television, only more efficiently and with instantaneous results. Digital media marketing outlets are particularly good at targeting specific audiences, gathering data, and building relationships. The ever-changing digital marketing realm begins with the channels I discuss next.

Content Marketing

By definition, content marketing is a type of marketing that involves the creation and sharing of online content, such as videos, blogs, and social media posts, that does not explicitly promote a brand but is intended to stimulate interest in its products or services. Content marketing drives traffic to a company's website, helps a company convert that traffic into leads, demonstrates a company's expertise, and aides in driving a company's long-term results.

Social Media. Whether it's through social media platforms such as Facebook and Twitter or through other chosen channels, the establishment of a social media presence is increasingly important. Most social media platforms enable food brands to engage with consumers and have built-in data analysis tools, which enable companies to track the progress, success, and engagement of a campaign. Effective use of social media platforms also encourages user-generated content when consumers post their own content that focuses on a company's products.

Search Engine Marketing. Leveraging the strength of digital's highly targetable and cost-efficient model, search engine marketing and strategic branded banner ad placement offers the ability to get your campaign in front of consumers in desktop, laptop, or mobile browsers after they've conducted a search tied to a keyword your campaign is bidding for. This means, instead of general ads for products they have no interest in at that time, they see contextually relevant ads about products they have been researching for on sites they visit for news or entertainment.

Digital Radio and Streaming Services. Straddling traditional radio and social media are digital radio and streaming services like Pandora and Spotify. These services offer the same highly targetable, cost-efficient, and trackable options afforded on most online marketing platforms. These services also are superior to the traditional "radio spot" format by adding clickable banner ads to the app that takes the consumer to an actionable offer on their mobile, laptop, or desktop browser.

Blogs. A marketing blog is an interactive and frequently updated website or web page that is usually attached to a company's primary website. In the food industry, this might mean recipes and cooking or lifestyle tips. Blogging has become a great way for a business to improve a company's search engine optimization, increase website traffic, and demonstrate expertise.

Online Videos. Online videos are emerging as an ideal way to capture the attention of consumers, many of whom prefer watching videos rather than reading content. Looking for recipe videos, anyone? As of this book's writing, Instagram and YouTube were perhaps the most popular online video platforms for the food industry.

Email. Email marketing that engages and cultivates a company's fan base and loyalty club is essential in the digital age. It can be considered the digital version of traditional direct marketing.

Websites and Search Engine Optimization. No matter what industry a company is in, its website is the hub of its business. The notion that a company should have a website is nothing new. However, it's no longer enough just to have a web presence. Companies need dynamic websites with fresh and frequently updated content that encourages people to revisit the site and remain engaged with the company and its brand.

Search engine optimization (SEO) is a useful tool to consider when developing and maintaining your website. SEO addresses a company's desire to rise in the ranks among search engine results, ideally climbing up to page one. Using strategic keywords, fresh content, and useful information on its website can help a company achieve this goal, and therefore, improve its chances for increased awareness and, theoretically, increased business.

TRADITIONAL MARKETING CHANNELS

Traditional marketing channels include billboards, newspapers, magazines, television, radio, and direct public interaction. Some of these channels may appear to be giving way to digital media channels, but they need to still be considered as part of a fully integrated strategic marketing plan.

Newspapers. One of the oldest marketing channels, newspapers provide daily advertising opportunities. The readership of most newspapers consists of people who are local to a specific area, enabling you to target specific geographic neighborhoods. The Sunday editions of most newspapers also provide an opportunity for you to partner with your retailers/buyers on free-standing inserts (FSIs), which automatically increase brand awareness with consumers when they are most likely to be in a shopping mode. Adding coupons to both the daily and Sunday newspapers further increases the likelihood of increased brand awareness, while also inviting a consumer to purchase your product on a "trial" basis and helping you track the effectiveness of your marketing efforts. Furthermore, the daily frequency of a newspaper publication offers a high level of flexibility in terms of marketing strategy.

Radio. Radio is an effective advertising avenue because even the weakest radio signals can reach a wide area, and its commercials are both brief and relatively inexpensive. Most American towns have their own radio stations, meaning a business can broadcast its messages as narrowly or broadly as it wishes, depending on its goals and budget. Like newspapers, radio offers the opportunity for flexible short-term advertising.

Billboards. One of the largest forms of traditional advertising, billboards are normally positioned along interstate highways or other high-traffic areas that are usually located near your business or one where your products are available. Billboards should be highly visible and carry short simple messages. The goal of billboard advertising is overall brand awareness, as opposed to call-to-action advertising that offers consumers special incentives to purchase specific products.

Magazines. Whereas newspaper advertising usually targets specific geographical regions, magazine advertising provides businesses with a chance to target potential consumers based on their interests. Magazines offer a similar, but longer-lasting, channel for traditional print advertising. Compared to daily newspaper advertising, which is as disposable as the newspaper itself, magazines are published less often but kept by consumers for longer periods. A magazine is also an attractive advertising format that is frequently passed on from person to person, meaning each advertisement is likely to be seen by multiple potential consumers.

Television. Once considered the ideal channel for marketing campaigns, television is still a powerful marketing avenue for those businesses that can afford it. In many ways, it's the ultimate vehicle for a company's visual identity. Television advertising is like radio advertising in that it reaches a broad audience and infuses a company and its brand with a measure of personality that is often unattainable through print advertising. Also like radio advertising, television advertising spots can be purchased during the times of day and days of the year that a company's target market is most likely to encounter them and act upon that encounter.

GRASSROOTS CHANNELS

Campaigning through grassroots channels can involve many different activities. It can include events like lectures, free samples and taste testing, festivals, fairs, grocery store demos, and food truck sales. Grassroots campaigns can also involve events and promotional tie-ins with local sports teams that compete on the high school, college, and professional levels, as well as telephone sweeps and the distribution of door hangers and fliers—anything that gets your company and its brand out there at the neighborhood level.

THE GOOD, THE BAD, AND THE COSTLY

Both digital and traditional media marketing campaigns have their advantages. Most companies depend on some combination of the two, and many new or small companies begin by utilizing just one or two channels in their marketing strategies. Which marketing channels you choose and how you choose to use them comes down to your goals, your budget, and your target market.

There are four key parts of marketing campaigns that must be considered as a company weighs the pros and cons of digital and traditional media outlets: price, target audience, timeliness, and access to information.

Price. Digital forms of advertising are frequently somewhat less expensive than traditional media buys. This is often a make-or-break factor, particularly for new and smaller businesses.

Target audience. Digital media tools and online campaigns tend to be much better at sifting through the demographics and psychographics of potential consumers—and ultimately reaching desired audiences—than traditional tools and channels.

Timeliness. Traditional advertising does not normally enable a company to respond to changes in the marketplace as quickly as digital media advertising. Whereas traditional campaigns take days or even weeks to develop, implement, and adjust, digital media campaigns can be altered in a matter of minutes.

Access to information. The message a company can deliver through traditional channels is much more limited than the message that can be delivered through digital media outlets. The message a company wants to convey is limited by time and space when it utilizes traditional marketing channels, but there are no such constraints on digital media channels. With digital media campaigns, interested consumers are a simple click away from an almost endless amount of additional information.

Your company's choice of marketing campaign channels ultimately depends on what kind of products you sell, what your message is, who your target market is, and how much money you want to spend. Not everybody watches traditional television, and newspaper readership has been steadily declining for the last decade. Then again, not everyone is constantly glued to their mobile phone. It's up to each company to determine which media channels are bound to be most effective for them.

OUR MARKETING MATRIX

As you develop a marketing campaign, it's important that you have a reliable way to judge its effectiveness. To do so, you must ask yourself a few fundamental questions. Is it conveying the essence of your brand message in the best way possible? Are you talking about what matters most to your audience? What's in it for them?

These are some loaded questions if your goal is to fight off the competition and attract consumers. To answer these questions, and potentially improve your campaign, NewPoint has developed over time a quantifiable system of measurement for the effectiveness of both existing campaign messages and the ones that we develop with our partners. We call it the Brand Affinity Matrix.

The Brand Affinity Matrix, as shown, is essentially a scorecard by which the message of a marketing campaign can be graded. The items listed on the horizontal axis (you/others/audience) represent "who" the ad is about, while the items on the vertical axis (ideas/things/people) represent "what" the ad is about.

It's our belief that those ads which come closest to reaching 100 on the scorecard are most likely to be effective. The delivery of a message through an advertisement that is about the audience (most often mom) and people (usually those that mom knows and loves) can send a consumer's affinity for your message through the roof. On the other hand, if a company's campaign ad is all about the company itself and its ideas, it has a strong chance of failing to resonate with consumers and being forgettable. Nobody wants to hear someone else talk about themselves all the time.

To provide more clarity to its workings, here's a breakdown of how we can gauge how effective a brand message is using our Brand Affinity Matrix scorecard:

NewPoint Brand Affinity Matrix

	audience	others	you
people	100	50	10
things	50	25	5
ideas	10	5	1

© 2017 NewPoint Marketing

Here's how we use this tool to measure brand affinity messaging:

NewPoint Brand Affinity Matrix

	audience	others	you
people	100	50	10
things	50	25	5
ideas	10	5	(1)

© 2017 NewPoint Marketing

If the message is about the company or brand and its big idea—"We're the best because we've been in business for 125 years"—the score range is typically 1 to 5 points.

If the message is about things such as the features and benefits of the product and it's endorsed by a third party—for instance, "Four out of five dentists recommend Trident for their patients who chew gum" or Beyoncé holding a Diet Pepsi—the score range is 25 to 50 points.

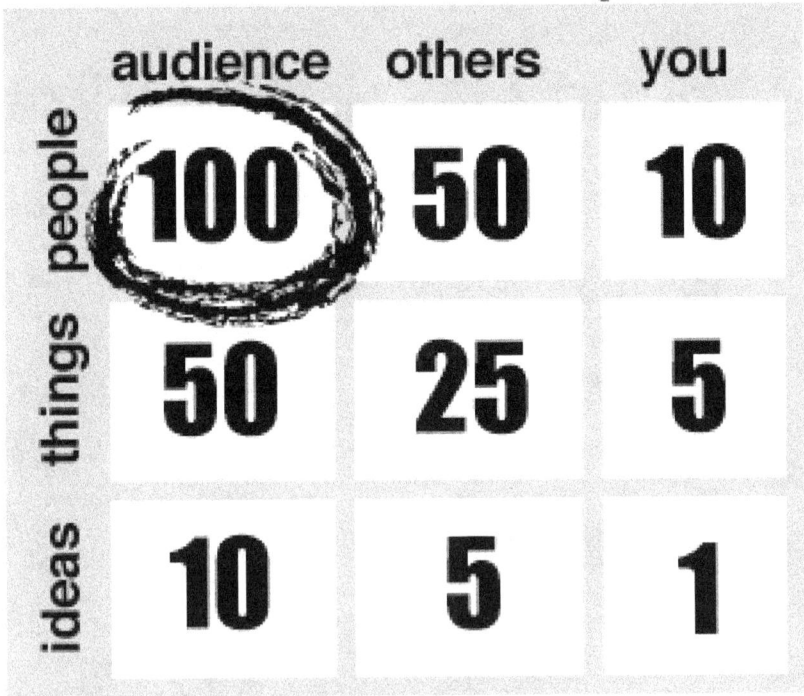

If the message is about the audience and the people they care about – famously illustrated in an outstanding Michelin ad that showed a baby sitting inside a tire laying on its side with the headline: You've Got a Lot Riding On Your Tires. You have great copy specifically directed at the target audience (Mom and Dad) and addresses what they care most about (children and family) – the score can be as high as 100 points.

NewPoint Brand Affinity Matrix

	audience	others	you
people	**(100)**	50	10
things	50	25	5
ideas	10	5	1

	audience	others	you
people	100	**(50)**	10
things	50	25	5
ideas	10	5	1

	audience	others	you
people	100	50	10
things	50	**(25)**	5
ideas	10	5	1

	audience	others	you
people	100	50	10
things	50	25	5
ideas	10	5	**(1)**

© 2017 NewPoint Marketing

A brand manager who truly knows what their target audience cares about should be able to develop brand messaging that scores at least 50 points on our scorecard.

I think we're all familiar with the famous Got Milk ad campaign. This creative scores a solid 50 for its testimonial ads – always the hottest celebrities and personalities (others/people), always promoting milk to their fan base, who (Milk hopes) will want to emulate them.

MEASURING AND ANALYZING YOUR CAMPAIGN

The Brand Affinity Matrix is a good starting point, but our focus is on the important roles data measurement, data analysis, and strategic adjustment play in your campaign strategies. Marketing campaigns are driven by data, so it's crucial for you to measure as many aspects of each campaign as possible. This includes the amount of money you spend on a campaign, which channels you utilize, how many consumer interactions you amass, and so on.

In the case of traditional marketing avenues, progress can be tracked through coupon redemption, sell-through results, and product reorders. Most digital media channels, as I've mentioned, already have built-in methods of tracking and analyzing marketing data. This data is, therefore, easy to attain. Another way to measure the success of any marketing campaign is by interacting with the consumers themselves through consumer surveys and focus groups.

Once you have gathered the necessary data, you should objectively analyze it to determine the effectiveness of each campaign, with the goal of improving your methods and adjusting them for future launches. Remember that the goal of each campaign is both increased brand awareness and a positive return on investment.

Your Campaign and Buyers/Retailers

Buyers and retailers can be viewed as playing three different roles when it comes to a company's marketing campaign. Their first role is that of a new customer target, where you are enticing new buyers/retailers to give you an opportunity to pitch your products to them. The next role is that of new partner target, where you are convincing the buyers/retailers to carry your products for resale in their retail outlets. The third role is that of partner, where you and your buyers/retailers work together to promote your products to the end-line consumers.

New-customer target. In many ways, buyers/retailers should be treated just like consumers, as you place ads in their trade magazines and target them through websites and other digital media channels. A company can also draw their attention at trade shows, where companies can increase brand awareness and forge relationships with buyers and retailers.

New partner target. Buyers and retailers will want to know about your company's entire marketing campaign, including both the digital and the traditional avenues you plan to pursue. Your level of investment is likely to be mirrored in their likelihood to commit to carrying your products.

Partnering. Partnering with buyers/retailers is a mutually beneficial relationship in which both parties commit to investing in promotions such as in-store demos, instantly redeemable coupons (IRCs), and co-branded FSIs. This partnership is crucial in the formation of ongoing relationships with any company's buyers and retailers.

CONCLUSION

From the multiple media outlets available to the look and tone of your message, you have a myriad of choices to make when it comes to your marketing campaigns. What combination of digital and traditional media outlets should you choose? Does your campaign convey the essence of your brand message in the best way possible? Consumer awareness, brand affinity, and growth are the goals and a return on investment wouldn't hurt, either. No matter what you choose, your campaigns must be thoughtful, flexible, and well-executed if you want to make your move.

Section 4

Brand Growth Programs

Chapter 11

BRAND MANAGEMENT

A war is being waged and the battlefield reaches from the internet to retail shelves. The winners of this war are awarded business, increased market share, and the profits that go with it. As consumers, we are the target. Every single item we purchase, from the soap we shower with to the food we eat to the toothpaste we brush our teeth with, has been strategically branded, positioned, and marketed specifically with us in mind.

Put another way, there's a person sitting in an office somewhere whose only professional reason for being is to get us to buy the brand they oversee instead of the competition. I am guessing they're sitting at a bank of computer monitors with point-of-sale, syndicated market data, and focus group and consumer trend data flowing by as the information is reflected in the lenses of their glasses.

The person driving that brand strategy? That's the brand manager. A company that understands the value of brand marketing will have a marketing staff—or engage a firm like NewPoint—to do the job of brand management. A brand manager's job is to manage the brand with the objective of gaining sales and market share. Of course, brand management is important in business-to-business marketing. However, it's dwarfed by consumer goods marketing, simply by the size of the target audience, the heat of the competition, and the amount of dollars at stake. That's where the fun begins.

A good consumer brand manager should know the target audience better than they know their own mother. Unless, of course, their mother is in the target audience. If that is the case, and it often is, mom will most likely find herself being asked seemingly random questions about her views on everything from bacon to breakfast cereal—whatever branded product it is that her son or daughter is managing.

The dollars at stake are such that it's not only businesses in the high-profile categories that have brand managers. Yes, Coke and Starbucks spare no expense to manage their brands and get their message in front of us. But every other branded product we interact with each day and across all product categories from laundry detergent, ballpoint pens, cookies, toothpaste, shirts, and gas stations are brand managed to win the sale. It's our belief that brand management is even more crucial in the food industry where margins are tight, the competition is stiff, and the marketplace itself is increasingly fragmented.

As a brand manager in numerous industries, I have been involved in focus groups and attitude/usage studies to better understand, among a multitude of other things, buying behavior, product usage, and brand perception, all separated demographically, geographically, and psychographically. It may seem like overkill, but it's done for the branded laundry detergent you bought last weekend and the branded ballpoint pen you are holding in that staff meeting.

A brand manager knows their target audience, what they care about, and how they shop. When a brand manager's brand is positioned correctly, it is ready to be marketed to their target audience. That means more than just working through cost of goods, pricing, margins, distribution, and the competitive landscape. To sell their product into the retail environment (even if their brand is not a Starbucks-caliber brand), a brand manager must think about numerous "brand" marketing building blocks, such as the brand voice, the brand look, the brand personality, and ultimately the branded campaign.

This is where NewPoint's Brand Affinity Matrix comes into play. As I mentioned previously, the whole point of the Brand Affinity Matrix is to obtain a quick internal measurement of branded messages and branded campaigns according to their ability to make emotional connections with individual consumers and those they care most about. Personal connections like these represent powerful ways to connect with shoppers and promote brand affinity. Brand affinity, in turn, can lead to all sorts of good things, including increased market share and profits.

In summation, a brand manager's job is to find the brand love and a market share will follow it. Let's now proceed to my professional take on the key components, processes, and responsibilities involved in effective brand management.

BRAND MANAGEMENT BASICS

By definition, brand management is the analysis and planning of how a brand is perceived in the market. Brand managers are primarily concerned with the creation of lasting impressions among consumers and improving product sales and market share through the proper development of a brand's image. Productive relationships with company employees, buyers/retailers, and the target market are essential for effective brand management.

In NewPoint's experience, the role of brand manager essentially amounts to a couple of lengthy grocery lists of how-to components and general responsibilities, which are listed next.

The Brand Management Process

* Identify and define the fundamental motivations of your target audience.
* Find an advantageous brand position—one that differentiates your product.
* Convert that position into a consistent and strong brand identity.

* Develop all aspects of your brand messaging.
* Educate employees about your brand identity and cultivate them as brand ambassadors.
* Develop a comprehensive and integrated marketing plan.
* Augment your brand's promise throughout all consumer interactions.
* Monitor the ongoing performance of your brand, adjusting it accordingly.

Brand Management Responsibilities

* Continually manage your brand's performance.
* Expand your brand awareness, differentiation, value, and consumer connectedness.
* Develop a comprehensive brand plan.
* Monitor the progress of and adjust the brand plan accordingly.
* Promote brand understanding and support throughout your organization.
* Drive initiatives that ensure delivery of your brand promise.
* Oversee all aspects of your brand messaging and its consistency.
* Discover and develop new brand opportunities.

These lists even include broad concepts like brand positioning and marketing plans that are far more complex than these lists suggest. Important details such as situation analysis, consumer demographics and psychographics, store checks, and campaign development, exist only between the lines here. In addition, there's the dreaded possibility of crisis, which calls for a very specific and extremely important type of brand management. NewPoint does all these things, and we work with clients that do all these things, too. Basically, every aspect of this book and every aspect of your company's potential growth involves brand management to some degree, so its importance cannot be overstated.

In fact, many large companies within the food industry have entire departments that are devoted to brand management—armies' full of analysts and managers. The truth is that most local, small, or regional food companies can't afford such luxuries, so they often hire outside companies (like NewPoint) to ensure the job is done properly. Either way, as the industry fractures and becomes more complex, effective brand management is becoming increasingly important for those companies that hope to grow and prosper.

The Keys to Success

There are several key items from the previously mentioned lists that brand managers must execute if they hope to be successful. These key items include both general practices as well as concepts that are increasingly important in the emerging arena of digital marketing. They are as follows:

Know your target audience. This should be obvious by now, but it always deserves a mention. A complex subject, knowledge of your target audience usually involves some combination of the mom factor, the 80/20 rule, and the rise of millennials.

Differentiate. Also a no-brainer, differentiation is crucial in a marketplace that is both crowded and fiercely competitive. Your product features should be different, your message should be unique, and your visual identity should be singularly appealing.

Keep it simple. While the attention span of your customers is shrinking and the volume of communications available to them is almost overwhelming, less is often more and simple is frequently better.

Remain consistent. All aspects of your branded message should remain consistent for the same reasons you must keep it simple. Cut through the crowd noise of the marketplace by sticking to your core message as much as possible.

Embrace technology. Technology has joined consumer insight, strategy, and creativity among the things driving brand management. Consumers experience brands through computers, mobile phones, and other technological devices more and more every day, which has led to an increasing number of marketing touch points. Learn how to use this fact to your advantage.

Bridge the digital divide. Connect your traditional and new media marketing channels under the umbrella of a cohesive strategy. Fractured brand experiences are a hindrance to your brand and its message.

Utilize social media and content marketing. Both emerging marketing channels are increasingly important ways to shape and develop your brand's online presence, which can increase brand awareness and draw consumers to your company's website.

COMMON BRAND MANAGEMENT MISTAKES

Brand management has clearly evolved into a multifaceted responsibility over recent years, and that increased responsibility can come with pitfalls. It's been NewPoint's experience that there are several avoidable mistakes that today's brand managers commonly make. They include:

Improper value proposition. A brand's value proposition sets customer expectations. Deciding on the right value proposition requires the thoughtful analysis of a brand's strengths and the target audience. Any misunderstanding of a brand's proposition can have a negative effect on the brand's image.

Lack of consistency. An inconsistent message can result in a brand campaign that's not memorable or is confusing. A company must find its identity, define its message, and be consistent about it across all the marketing outlets it chooses to utilize.

Disregarding analytics. Analytics has always been an important component of marketing, but its use is both more important and easier to access and utilize in the digital age. Taking advantage of analytics leads to better strategy development.

Disregarding social media. Social media as a marketing channel is both ubiquitous and critical. Ignoring or neglecting social media impedes a company's ability to connect with today's consumers, particularly at a grassroots level and with the emerging millennial generation.

Neglecting your online presence. A company cannot just establish a website, Facebook page, Twitter account, or blog outlet, and then forget about them. Neglected social media gives off an impression of a brand that isn't fully engaged, which can lead to negative impressions on the part of consumers. Do it right or don't do it at all.

Generic branding. Thanks to the online conveniences of the digital age, which offer companies inexpensive access to many marketing tools and creative work, marketing design may appear to be as easy as ever. However, this use of generic resources can lead to a misrepresented or completely forgettable message. Effective brand management requires careful consideration across all aspects of its brand message development.

MORE BRAND GROWTH PROGRAMS: AN OVERVIEW

Now that I've addressed the fundamentals of brand management, I'll discuss several specific brand growth strategies in the upcoming chapters within this section. I'll begin with brand activation and the building of a marketing plan. Then, I'll address the building of a regional powerhouse; embracing digital media; and developing loyalty programs, public relations, and crisis management; and strategic product development.

Chapter 12 focuses on brand activation and the building of a marketing plan. It includes activation strategies, of course, as well as consumer awareness tactics and brand engagement methods. Topics also include the employment of shopper marketing and both traditional and digital coupons. Finally, I'll address the organization and packaging of entire campaigns and marketing programs for presentation, while also discussing finances.

How a company goes about becoming a regional powerhouse will be the subject of Chapter 13. This includes goal identification and definition of a company's target region as well as the planning and forecasting of sales and marketing growth. Numerous growth methods will also be discussed, from inviting trial and partnering with buyers and retailers to digital marketing and grassroots tactics.

Chapter 14 focuses on digital media, loyalty programs, and the evolving relationship between a brand and its consumers. This includes the establishment of a digital personality, the setting of digital marketing rules, social media engagement, and the emergence of social media as a customer service platform. Coverage on the importance and cultivation of a loyalty club is also included.

Chapter 15 discusses public relations and crisis management. The establishment of an ongoing program of favorable public relations, including grassroots strategies, is followed by a comprehensive guide to best practices when unforeseen or otherwise unfortunate events take place.

Chapter 16 focuses on strategic product development and includes discussions about product innovation, ideal customer identification, and trend and category analysis. This chapter also addresses all the facets of the product development process.

Chapter 12

BRAND ACTIVATION

When my team and I talk about the role of marketing in your food production business, one of our go-to, big-picture metaphors involves what we call the three-legged stool. It usually goes something like the following.

LEG ONE IS MARKETING.

The marketing leg of the stool represents the process of creating brand awareness and finding marketing opportunities. It positions your company and its food brand by differentiating it from the competition, highlighting its unique features and benefits, and developing an effective call-to-action for setting up sales and bringing in leads. In a best-case scenario, good advertising reaches the qualified and most coveted target audience, creating a brand preference. In short, turn advertising on to drive your target market toward sales. Note, if the marketing leg of the stool works too hard, sales may not have the capacity to convert.

LEG TWO IS SALES.

The sales leg of the stool represents the process of delivering on the brand promise that the first leg, marketing, has made. The sales leg validates that the target market is, indeed, a potential customer and that they value the brand and the company for the right reasons. Sales also confirms that your company and its brand can deliver what the target market is looking for at a fair price. Furthermore, sales are responsible for ensuring that both the buyer and the end-line consumer receive the correct message. Ideally, sales does more than convert your target market into a one-time customer. The goal is to convert it into a recurring and long-term customer. In short, you must inspire sales to drive the target market to sales conversion. Note, if the sales leg of the stool works too hard, operations may not have the capacity to convert.

LEG THREE IS OPERATIONS.

The operations leg of the stool represents the process of getting your branded food product to the new customer, therefore delivering on the promise that sales made to your new customer. This obviously comes down to production capacity. The buyers need to know that you can deliver the goods and support restocks, but it's more than simply keeping up with orders. Operations must also deliver the quality and customer service levels that directly tie back into the brand promise made by your marketing and sales legs of the stool.

In this metaphor of the three-legged stool, all three legs—marketing, sales, and operations—must work in concert to act as a platform for growing your food production business. If even one leg does not operate properly, then the stool collapses—your company falters and you could potentially lose business and your market share as a result. If operations and sales aren't properly aligned with marketing, then time and money are bound to be wasted.

The three-legged stool concept is a good metaphor to keep in mind as you build your marketing plans and develop your food brand's activation strategies. The development process also requires a firm understanding of your company's overall plans and goals, which has been discussed at length before, but will briefly addressed again here. In this chapter, I'll also discuss the development of a plan that supports aggressive "turns" and both brand awareness and brand engagement tactics.

MARKETING AND ACTIVATION BASICS

There are several fundamental factors that should always be kept in mind as you develop your brand activation program. They touch on topics such as reach, money, and growth.

Intended reach. Determine how many consumers your brand activation plan should reach and how you intend to reach them. You should decide if your program is national, regional, or local in scope. You also must choose which media channels offer optimum ways to reach your target audience.

Relevance. Make sure that your brand activation program conveys your brand's core message and differentiates it from your competition. Ideally, your activation programs will integrate with all other aspects of your marketing and business plans.

Scalability. Is your brand activation program flexible enough to adjust to potential increases or decreases, depending on its ongoing progress? You must plan for growth and prepare for the opposite.

Return on investment. While all brand activation programs are not strictly measured in terms of sales made and dollars earned, you should be able to track a plan's costs and benefits. Profits made, market share earned, turns on shelves increased, data captured, and consumer feedback collected are all returns on investment as brand activation programs are designed to promote lasting consumer engagement.

Marketing Plans and Goals

Above all, the primary purpose of any marketing plan is to sell products and grow its market share. To get there, you must engage with your target audience and create brand awareness, invite trial, encourage the audience's continued usage, and develop brand affinity through product differentiation. Your plan should already be solidified, based on all the previous work you and your company have done, which includes comprehensive market analysis and positioning research. The goals you set for your brand should be well-defined, measurable, and realistic. In many ways, the remainder of your marketing plan depends on three things: time, target, and money.

You need to take your time as you consider the marketing options available to you within the brand activation space. Which marketing channels are best for your brand? Which tactics are most likely to reach your target market and offer you the best return on investment? How much are you realistically able to spend on your marketing plan? In addition, it's also important to remember that your marketing plans themselves take time to develop and mature after they are launched. Long-term relationships with your consumers are just as important, if not more important, than immediate sales, so it's crucial that you take your time to get your marketing plan right from the start and then let it run its course.

Supporting Turns and Sell-Through

Brand activation, by definition, is the art of driving consumer action through brand interaction and brand experiences. The goal of this consumer action is to invite brand trial, gain brand awareness, build brand popularity, and ultimately provide consumers with the kind of emotional experiences that make them feel personally connected to your brand. Effective brand activation programs can introduce new product lines, revitalize stagnating brands, reinforce brand positioning, and increase overall brand awareness.

The buyers we interviewed regularly stated that many manufacturers seem to believe that their only job is to get products on the shelves, which couldn't be further from the truth. Manufacturers like you also have the responsibility of moving these products after they hit the shelves. The ultimate purpose of brand activation is the production of what industry insiders call turns. Turns refer to the number of times your inventory is replaced or "turned over" by your buyers/retailers. Turns at the buyer/retailer level result from sales at the consumer level, and you want your turns to happen as fast as possible because a higher turn rate makes it difficult for your buyers/retailers to displace your brand with a competing product. Ideally, it's your brand that does the displacing. To support turns and sell through at the register, you must market to both your retailers and your consumers. As defined by kpilibrary.com, sell-through is a percentage of units sold during a period and it is calculated by dividing the number of units sold by the beginning on-hand inventory in a given time period.

MARKETING TO CONSUMERS

Television spots, radio plugs, event sponsorship, and all the other methods of brand awareness and engagement are important if you can afford them. However, the most cost-effective and foundational way to support turns and sell through is by marketing directly to consumers. This is ground zero of your brand's introduction, invitation to trial, and awareness building. The two basic tactics for marketing to consumers are shopper marketing and aggressive couponing.

Shopper Marketing

You've already read about the impulsive nature of a typical consumer's shopping behavior. According to a consumer buying habits study conducted by the Point-of-Purchase Advertising Institute and the Meyers Research Center, a full 70 percent of purchasing decisions are made in-store, and 68 percent of in-store purchases are based on impulse. This adds up to a lot of impulse buying, which is where shopper marketing comes into play.

As previously mentioned, shopper marketing involves making all last-minute appeals to consumers when they are standing at the shelf and deciding on a purchase. Shopper marketing can take many forms, including shelf-mounted coupon machines, shelf signs, floor graphics, and point-of-purchase promotions like case dividers and end cap displays. Shopper marketing also includes the use of coupons added to mobile phone retail apps and redeemed at the store, a process that is growing exponentially due to convenience and instant redeem ability. In fact, according to retaildive.com, spending through mobile coupons is expected to grow from $5.4 billion in 2012 to $43 billion by the end of 2017.

It's important to remember that shopper marketing does not have to be an overwhelming, all-or-nothing proposition. How and when you choose to employ shopper marketing tactics depends on your budget, your brand strategies, and your brand position.

Couponing

Couponing is a relatively inexpensive and scalable way to drive trial use, encourage continued purchase, and increase overall brand awareness. In all their variations, coupons are the bread and butter of traditional marketing. While the popularity of traditional media has declined, newspapers and magazines are still read by tens of millions of people daily. According to the Retail Feedback Group, 50 percent of all shoppers read printed circulars to find deals when planning a visit to the supermarket, 32 percent clipped coupons, and 25 percent read a printed in-store circular.

Free-standing inserts (FSIs), along with daily newspapers and other periodicals, are a highly effective channel for coupons. Valassis RedPlum and News America Marketing are the primary producers of FSIs, which normally appear in the Sunday editions of many newspapers. In fact, the Newspaper Association of America estimates that FSIs still reach some 50 million households nationwide each weekend, when most consumers are in prime shopping mode. One great aspect of FSIs, apart from the fact that they are inexpensive and scalable, is that they are designed and sold so that you can narrow your campaign's focus down to specific zip codes. Direct-mail circulars, which are a close cousin to FSIs, also carry the same benefits.

Coupons available through traditional media outlets aren't the only couponing tactics available to you, either. Instant redeemable coupons (IRCs), which are coupons that are affixed directly to the products themselves, encourage immediate trial with zero planning on the part of the consumer. The placement of these coupons directly in each consumer's shopping cart or basket has the same effect. There are also digital coupons, which consumers can access online or through social media outlets.

Marketing to Retail Buyers

In many ways, it's just as important to market your brand to your retail buyers as it is to market your brand to consumers. Your retail buyers are the gatekeepers to the marketplace and are, therefore, your first customers. With that in mind, you need to know what they want as you present your branded marketing plan to them. Buyers want to know that you have a comprehensive and well-funded plan based on your expertise in your category, and they want to know that you are willing to develop a lasting and mutually beneficial partnership with them. It's also important to remember that you are competing with other companies for their time, money, and limited shelf space.

Retail buyers want to familiarize themselves with your entire marketing plan, including your detailed plans for marketing to consumers. Your level of knowledge and investment in that area is likely to influence your buyer/marketer's decision to work with you. You can show even further commitment and attract more buyers and retailers by advertising in industry trade magazines.

As far as marketing directly to your buyers, you simply want your plan to appear polished and complete. The materials you take to your presentations should include, among other things, a branded product guide, a concise presentation, and a company overview brochure. Be mindful of the fact that quality and clarity is more important than quantity when it comes to your presentation materials. You should also remember that, unlike consumers, retail buyers are concerned about such components as marketing schedule, channel area, available advertising dollars, and promotional partnerships, as well as flexibility, production capacity, bulk purchases, and packaging durability. Be prepared to address these factors.

Many of the buyers and managers I spoke with for this book also expressed a strong desire to build fruitful long-term relationships with the people and companies they partner with. Ideally, they want everyone involved to succeed, and that requires a productive two-way partnership. They want to know if your company is capable of innovating, handling growth, and adapting to changes in the marketplace. The development of this relationship type is likely to lead to a true partnership, where you join together for brand development as well as co-branded promotions. Your ability to show that you are willing to partner goes a long way in swaying retail buyers.

Brand Awareness

By definition, brand awareness refers to the extent to which consumers are familiar with the distinctive qualities or image of a brand of goods or services. Brand awareness programs essentially function as extensions of your foundational brand activation plan. And, like your broader activation strategies, which awareness tactics you choose to utilize depends heavily on your overall goals, your target market, and your budget. Food, in general, is a necessary sort of goods, making it important to consumers across every demographic and psychographic category. For your branded products, the awareness tactics you might choose comes down to these three questions: Who's the target market? What's the right vehicle? And, what's it going to take to reach my target?

Who's the Target Audience?

As previously mentioned, finding your target audience involves geographic, psychographic, and demographic analyses. You wouldn't sell baby food to a single childless woman in her forties would you? No, because it's not for them. The same idea applies to brand awareness. You wouldn't advertise your product to people who aren't located within your target market, would you? No, although I've seen it happen plenty of times. An effective brand awareness strategy is framed around your target audience.

What's the Right Vehicle?

Soccer moms don't drive all four of their kids to practice in a two-seater Porsche, do they? No, because it's not practical. It's also impractical to think you're going to drive hundreds of consumers to your branded product using the wrong type of advertising. The sheer number of options available when it comes to brand awareness tactics, from the internet and social media to television and radio, can feel overwhelming. In addition, sales reps from each medium are constantly hounding you about the benefits of their vehicle, never thinking about your product's branded message or your target market. Be sure to match your advertising medium to your product's brand message.

What's It Going to Take to Reach My Target?

Every business owner wants to grow their business as expeditiously as possible. Brand awareness advertising can be expensive, and no company can afford to launch an awareness campaign that's both inefficient and ineffective. Regardless of your budget, a skilled media strategist should be able to find the right advertising tactics that best fit your target audience and craft a media plan that leverages all your options for optimum exposure. I've never talked to a business owner who was not concerned with the most ROI from their marketing investment.

Brand Awareness Tactics

As I've stated, different avenues are available to you for marketing purposes, including traditional media, digital media, and grassroots tactics. Each one has its advantages and disadvantages. It should be noted, however, that Market Track analysis has found that 80 percent of shoppers say they utilize more than one promotional media type to make purchase decisions, with print and websites being the most frequently used promotional vehicles.

Digital media. Includes websites, email, and other internet-based media. Compared to traditional media outlets, these outlets are better for finding your target audience and are easily measurable. Digital media is also growing as a brand awareness platform.

Traditional media. Includes television, radio, print, billboards, and point-of-purchase promotions. These methods can potentially reach a broad and diverse audience, but they're not as effective as digital media outlets at reaching specific target markets. They can also be expensive and difficult to measure when it comes to their effectiveness.

Grassroots tactics. These types of activities often overlap and spill into other aspects of your overall brand activation strategy. For the purposes of brand awareness, grassroots tactics include public relations (PR) and social media strategies. PR will be discussed at length in a later chapter, but it starts with strategic community involvement through cause marketing. Social media tactics, which are often misunderstood and misused, are an emerging component of the ongoing maintenance of your brand's identity, message, voice, and commitment.

Social Media and Brand Awareness

Marketing isn't social media, and social media alone is not marketing. Social media may represent an important component of an integrated and comprehensive marketing program, but it rarely works without a solid foundation. Social media should be utilized to support and help drive a brand's underlying marketing strategy and activation plan, and therefore, it should be viewed strategically.

There is one golden rule for social media and posting frequency: always be consistent. It may mean starting slowly with one tweet or Facebook post per day or one blog per month, but the idea is to keep producing content on a regular basis. Regularity helps you monitor the tone of your message, keep your brand engaged, and track the effectiveness of your posts based on retweets and shares. In fact, this last factor is the key to social media—dialing in to exactly what content to post and when to post it.

How much you rely upon social media marketing depends on the target. Experience, motivation, and trustworthiness—not age or inherent tech savvy—should determine who is in charge of your brand's social media program. You may want some of your young members on the team, but you don't necessarily want to name them team captain unless they are locked into your brand's foundational messaging. Finally, you want to consider how truly social you want your social media plan to be. Your plan should not be all business, all the time, nor should it be used as a one-way broadcast platform like television or newspapers. Your company can interact with your customers in a welcoming and engaging fashion once you've got some brand voice rules firmly in place and a schedule set.

The complete role of social media as a part of your brand's marketing plan will be discussed in an upcoming chapter.

Brand Engagement

Brand engagement plans can be essential to the creation of brand experiences, which are vital in producing a bona-fide emotional connection between you and your customers. As I've discussed, many of these activities can sometimes be part of your broader grassroots strategies. They help drive home the process of brand awareness, product trial, brand affinity, and brand loyalty.

Reinforce strategic community involvement and gain favor in the public eye by sponsoring an event focusing on a cause that's important to both you and your community. If you can afford to sponsor and/or host an event or festival, do it. Otherwise, ensure your brand is well-represented when events like these take place. Offer in-store samples, develop unique promotional activities, and establish a loyalty club. In fact, concepts like loyalty programs are so important that I've devoted much of Chapter 14 to them.

CONCLUSION

After all the homework, footwork, artwork, and planning are finished, the success of your company and its brand ultimately comes down to getting your branded product into the hands, mouths, minds, and hearts of the consumers. It's what first-class marketing plans and activation strategies are designed to do. From marketing to retail buyers and consumers to brand awareness and engagement tactics, you should be ready for your launch.

Chapter 13

REGIONAL BRAND POWERHOUSE

> *"As a national supplier, you kind of lose touch with the retailer. There's no way they can know the regional market. The biggest thing I know is, if you're a local supplier, you're shopping in those stores. You know the meat manager and you might even know the independent store owner. You know your customers, and your customers are in the area. You know what they want. All you have to do is figure out a way to spread the heads-up."*
>
> —J. D., buyer, 27 years' experience

Grocery stores can tell you a lot about the communities they're located in. Every town in every region of the country has a slightly different blend of stores. Each of these different stores have a different blend of products, including generic items, national staples, and regional and local specialties. In addition, every different region has its food powerhouses.

Whenever I travel around the country, I like to perform shelf checks everywhere I stop to visit. From the Food Lion in North Carolina to the Price Chopper in New York City, I've visited regional grocery stores all over the country to check their shelves and noted branded inventory for future reference. I like to pinpoint the regional food brands and gauge their geographic boundaries. I ask myself these questions: What kind of reach does that one regional brand have? What replaces it on the shelves once that reach has ended? When I do that, I'm taking the temperature of regional brands.

It's a matter of fact that in the not-too-distant past almost everything about America was regional, including food brands. National food brands were a rarity. Then, thanks in large part to twentieth-century advances in transportation and food preservation technology, the country became a far more connected place. One result of these advances was the birth of national food juggernauts.

My point here is that many of the brands we now think of as heavy hitters in the food industry started as small local businesses in an era when being a regional powerhouse was the goal. They often started out with the goal of only owning their backyard, which is a good goal to have.

BUILDING A REGIONAL POWERHOUSE

The easiest and most effective way to launch the expansion of your company and its brand is to begin selling more to your current customers. To do so, you need to set a template for going deep and planning wide, fully saturating your existing market. Doing so requires a plan. You need to identify your goals, define your target region or base, and then plan for overall growth, expansion of your marketing strategies, and an increase in production.

Define Your Region or Base

To grow, you must first define the region from which you will grow. Where does your brand currently have traction? It's most often in the region immediately surrounding your existing production area, but that may not always be the case. Either way, you must establish the focal point of your growth and proceed from there.

The phrase *focal point* is useful here because one of the simplest ways to establish your intended regions of growth is by marking them geographically on a map, with concentric circles extending outward from your established base. Simply place a pin on the map at the heart of your base region (or focal point), determine the radial distance for the first phase of your intended expansion, then draw a circle around that focal point. Here's an example from a recent NewPoint client:

The client was a food manufacturer based in the Indianapolis area. They placed a pinpoint on their plan where their plant was located and stated that they would like to establish their region within a 150-mile radius around that plant, which was a good start. However, when they drew their circle, it became apparent that their initial goal was probably too bold. That 150-mile radius included Indianapolis, which was not an unreachable target, but it also came close to including Chicago, Cincinnati, and even St. Louis and Detroit. Those cities are actually second- or third-phase targets in their growth plan—markets that should be tackled in the future. The solution was to decrease the initial radius of growth, pulling it in tighter, so that the first phase of expansion included an achievable goal. That aggressive initial radius of 150 miles became something tangible to shoot for as a part of their long-term goal.

This example is useful for two reasons: First, it lays out an effective way for you to establish your base region. Second, it reveals the importance of planning for and forecasting your future growth.

MARKET FOR GROWTH

Your marketing goal as you strive to become a regional powerhouse should be to encourage consumer trial of your products and gain ownership of your backyard through marketing and grassroots tactics. Getting your products on the shelves is just the beginning of the growth process. Your plan for marketing growth is directly linked with your overall plan as you partner with your retailers to grow together.

Your marketing plan should allow for changes in both budget and tactics as your overall plan develops. While you have a grand vision for your brand, your initial marketing plan for growth should start at home with the basics. Operating this way enables you to remain flexible and keep your precious marketing budget in check.

The difference between a general marketing plan and a marketing plan designed specifically for those companies that are shooting for regional powerhouse status is a difference in focus and intensity. General suggestions become requirements. Concepts become mandates. Ideas become reality. With that in mind, you need to flood your local and regional marketplaces with your brand and its message through digital, traditional, and grassroots marketing tactics.

Media Marketing Tactics

Utilizing media marketing tactics is the bread-and-butter way to reach your bread-and-butter audience. Ramp up your digital marketing campaign and focus that highly targetable channel on your regional audience. This campaign should include emails to your brand's loyalty club members and other fans, as well as social media promotion through Facebook, Twitter, Instagram, and other social media. Increase your regional point-of-purchase and shopper marketing efforts, including shelf signs, instantly redeemable coupons, end-cap displays, in-store product demos, and so on. Take advantage of the fact that FSIs are designed to target specific zip codes and carve up the geography of your target market. If possible, fill local and regional print publications with coupons and land prime radio and television advertising slots. Rent a billboard out by the highway or at the edge of town for advertising. Simply put, get the word out that you are in the game to win it.

Grassroots Marketing Tactics

Making a legitimate and lasting emotional impression on your target audience is an important part of any marketing plan, but it's crucial when you're talking about your own backyard. Select a worthy charitable cause, one that's important to both you and your community, and host events that promoting that cause and your connection to it. Join the local chamber of commerce. Sponsor, host, or otherwise take part in any and every local festival you can find. Cater local events and partner with local restaurants for co-sponsored brand experiences. Partner with college and professional sports organizations in your region for sponsorships and tie-ins. Do whatever you can to weave your company name and its brand into the fabric of your local communities and the collective psyche of its residents through meaningful personal interactions.

Leverage Local Brand Awareness

Intensifying your regional marketing should lead to a high awareness level for your brand as a local brand, both with consumers and with the folks responsible for stocking grocery shelves. It should also lead to increased brand loyalty, high sell-through, and turns on the shelves in your backyard or chosen home region.

When NewPoint talks to big fans of a branded product line the first thing we hear is, "Do they make anything else?" In later chapters, I'll discuss new product development strategy in detail, but the conversation starts right here in your backyard. Consumer are primed and asking for more products and, as our buyer interviews tell us, retailers understand the importance of building on success, especially if a new product line is a logical extension of your current successful line.

Leverage your consumer fan base to discuss and test new product line ideas. Find out what they are they looking for. Get into the stores and see what competitive products you can target. Partner with a retailer for small-run product testing ,which you can support with targeted marketing, to get a read on a product's viability while minimizing exposure.

Adding line extensions—different pack sizes, flavors, and price points—and strategically adding new products can have a big impact on your business's bottom line. It can also improve your relationship with the retailers and increase consumer loyalty because they can now buy more of your brand.

CONCLUSION

Perhaps the best way to sum up what it means to become a true regional powerhouse comes from an observation made by one of the buyers I interviewed for this project:

> *"Let's go back to that smaller local company. I'll use a manufacturer, let's say it's Brand X. They built their whole company around hot dogs. There is brand awareness when somebody goes in and sees Brand X hot dogs. Now, if you go to a retailer in Brand X's market and you look at their hot dog display case, there are four, five facings of Brand X hot dogs. All kinds of different varieties and packages. All the other competitors in that area are fighting to get one slot, one row. Brand X has developed a brand awareness on that one, and then they've branched out and moved into sausages or whatever. You get that local brand awareness where people say, 'Oh dear, their hot dogs are the best.' Then, suddenly, a consumer sees another product, where they've got a sausage or a bratwurst. The consumers, they relate to it. 'Oh yeah, the hot dog was good. This bratwurst has to be good, too.'"*
>
> —M. L., buyer, 16 years' experience

Chapter 14

GET DIGITAL AND GROW THE BRAND

Social media is one of the biggest topics in business today. Even though it's a hot topic, it's still something that many companies are slow to take advantage of and utilize. As a marketing guy, I talk to a lot of people about brand, market share, and the topic of social media. Here is one question I often get asked: "Is marketing on social media that much different than traditional marketing?" My answer, "Yes and no."

YES: Social media is a maturing, measurable, and credible communications platform that's all about being a brand and being social. Social media is doing nothing less than defining the future of how brands engage. It means engagement with anyone and everyone who wants to tweet about a brand, become a fan of a brand, add a brand to their Pinterest page, or tag branded videos on YouTube.

NO: As an emerging discipline, social marketing is no different from traditional marketing in that it still needs to be strategically integrated with an organization's brand message, communications platform, and overall corporate mission. Also, much of social media marketing is about engaged communication and building relationships, which sounds very much like any successful business relationship I have ever been involved with.

My team and I have developed a few guidelines to help companies start down the right path towards effective social media marketing. Let's begin!

ESTABLISH A VOICE, A PERSONALITY, AND SOME RULES

The most common question I hear about starting a Twitter account, posting blogs, and utilizing other similar social media tools is, "What should I write about?" That's a complicated question. For companies like yours, I typically suggest going back to the cornerstone of your communications platform: your brand positioning. It's a good place to begin the process of building the base rules for your online brand voice because brand positioning should always define how your company's brand is relevant to its target audience in relation to the competition.

An organization with a well-defined brand position can, with a little work (and help from their favorite strategic marketing firm), set up rules to help define the brand's personality—what the brand stands for, cares about, posts about—and how it responds and engages with followers, friends, and fans who post on their social media sites.

EMBRACE THE PROCESS WITH A PLAN

In many ways, marketing is a process. No one I know produces a television spot, print ad, internet banner ad, billboard ad, or any other communication tool and then runs it only once. In fact, you must give a lot of strategic thought about your target audience, what your company wants the audience to know or do, and when the audience should encounter the communication. Then, the metrics are measured for effectiveness, perhaps tweaked in some way, and launched again.

The same goes for marketing on social media. With a larger strategic marketing plan in place, your social media program should support and enhance your brand and/or campaign messaging. As mentioned previously in the discussion on brand activation in Chapter 12, social media alone is not marketing and it rarely works without a solid foundation.

I also spoke about the fundamentals of social media marketing in Chapter 12. In short, you must develop a regular posting schedule and remain consistent about it. Figure out what content and frequency of posting works best for you based on consumer response. Don't just hand your social media marketing operations to the youngest person on your staff because they use their smartphone more than you do. Treat your social media marketing plan like the pivotal tool it is, and assign responsibility based on experience, motivation, and marketing knowledge.

ENGAGE TO BUILD CREDIBILITY, RELATIONSHIPS, AND COMMUNITY

A brand exists to grow and expand your market share. Social media presents a great opportunity to support this mission in a tangible, trackable, and integrated way.

Not many people can get away with calling themselves an expert. That said, you are an expert in your product niche, and expert-quality content can be demonstrated in posts that are relevant to the audience and differentiate your brand relative to the competitive landscape. Credibility, like trust, is built post by post.

What happens when someone responds, retweets, shares, or even challenges a post? What happens when someone complains on your brand's Facebook, Twitter, or Google reviews page? Your brand needs to engage and respond quickly.

Think about your typical business meeting and all the niceties that are exchanged before everyone gets down to work. Usually when folks arrive at a business meeting, the first few minutes are spent exchanging a little personal information. Personally, I like to know about the people I am doing business with, so I ask about their weekend, their kids, their hobbies, etc. This is a good analogy for how social media marketing for a brand works: we do business with people we like. Social media users are people who are fans or followers of brands they like. You should, therefore, treat them with courtesy and respect. It's easy to respond with a simple "thanks" or "way to go" to a fan post, but social media interaction can also be a very effective way to handle a complaint. We recently saw this happen first-hand on the Facebook page of one of our clients.

A complaint was lodged on the client's Facebook page by a consumer who was trying to buy our client's product. Apparently, the customer had a bad experience with our client's coupon at a retailer. Our social media marketing staff saw the complaint and alerted the right people in our client's organization. Our client made a call to the supermarket, and that company jumped onto our client's Facebook page and handled the problem with a sincere apology and a gift.

This all happened in its entirety within a few hours on a Saturday afternoon. The response on our client's Facebook page was overwhelmingly positive. Not only was the complaint dealt with and the "fan" made happy, but, judging by the "likes" on that exchange over the next day or so, a lot of other fans of the brand appreciated what they saw, too.

This is a good example of our guidelines for social media marketing in action. Responses to fan posts should be timely and in context with the corporate brand mission—making the customer happy. The happiness of your customers is also the point of your overall digital marketing and brand loyalty programs as they are crucial parts of your brand's mission and its public engagement.

Getting Digital

Digital Media by the Numbers

Nielsen released the "2016 Nielsen Social Media Report Social Studies: A Look at The Social Landscape", which focused on social media behavior among consumers, and the results were revealing. Perhaps the most important findings were that members of Generation X (ages 35–49) spend more time than millennials (ages 25–34) on social media and that the use of multiple devices at once is now considered to be commonplace. Here's a summary of the Nielsen findings:

* Members of Generation X spend nearly seven hours per week on social media, compared to just over six hours per week for millennials.
* Women spend more of their online time on social media (25 percent) than men (19 percent).
* Among heavy users who spend more than three hours per day on social media, 39 percent believe that researching products and services is an important reason for using social media.
* Among heavy users, 29 percent find that supporting their favorite companies or brands somewhat to very important.
* In terms of simultaneous multiple-platform usage, 30 percent of smartphone users and 21 percent of tablet users said they used those devices while watching television.
* Among those who used multiple devices at once, 58 percent of smartphone users and 57 percent of tablet users said they visited Facebook while they watched television. Those numbers dropped to 20 and 24 percent, respectively, when it came to Twitter.

* In general, Nielsen concluded that Generation X women of all cultural categories are most likely to be using their smartphones or tablets to access Facebook on Sundays while watching television.

There you have it—the tried-and-true mom rule holds. Television still makes an impact. Not only do consumers use social media as a gateway to product information, they have a very real desire to voice support for their favorite companies and brands through social media.

Leveraging the Numbers

The numbers make it clear that taking part in social media is a crucial component of a growing company's marketing plan. As mentioned earlier in this chapter, it's important to engage in consumer relationships and make the customer happy through social media. There are several ways to go about it. Basically, the idea is to humanize your brand, think of the customers you deal with through social media as if they were friends of the brand, and have genuine communications with them. Some of the ways to do this include the following:

* Develop a unique written voice and use everyday language.
* Engage in interactive conversations with your customers when they have comments.
* Acknowledge mistakes and offer solutions.

Just as you should imagine each consumer as an individual person, you should present your company as a collection of individual people. This process can begin with social media where authentic personal engagement is the name of the game.

Social Media and Customer Service

It's becoming increasingly obvious that social media is the go-to communications platform for companies of all sizes, and as I showed you before, customer service is a significant part of that communication. Dealing with customer complaints through social media has become the new normal, bypassing the traditional customer service departments at many companies. However, a pair of recent reports indicate that customer service sought through social media channels has been inadequate at best.

Recent customer experience reports overseen by customer relations services Harris Interactive and RightNow found that 26 percent of U.S. adults expressed frustration after a poor experience by posting a negative comment on social media, and that 79 percent of those complaints went unanswered. A 2017 report by social media marketing analysts at Spredfast, which focused on the consumer-packaged goods industry, proved to be even more disappointing. According to that report, which only drew from Twitter interactions, consumer packaged goods companies left a whopping 91 percent of tweets concerning customer service unanswered.

Considering that Harris Interactive/RightNow also reported that companies potentially lose as much as 20 percent of annual revenue due to poor customer experiences, good customer service, which is increasingly the job of social media managers. is mandatory. An effective social media customer service plan should be developed, including plans for maintaining, tracking, and improving customer service overall. If you want to improve your social media customer service, be strategic about it. Set realistic goals for increasing the number of complaints answered. Develop a system that helps you prioritize these complaints according to immediacy and importance, remembering that response quality can matter more than response quantity.

Website Strategies

Although social media is the rage right now, it doesn't mean you should neglect your company's primary website. On the contrary, many of the marketing strategies and tactics laid out within this book are meant to funnel consumers to your website. It's the ultimate source of your company's story, product information, and perhaps most importantly, coupons and other promotions.

According to a 2017 Food Marketing Institute (FMI) study of shopper trends, the number of consumers who say they at least occasionally shop online for groceries increased from 20 percent to 25 percent over the course of the previous year. That number skyrocketed from 28 percent to 43 percent among millennials, a change FMI referred to as a "tipping point." The report also stated that consumer-packaged goods are among the products that consumers are most likely to research and buy online. Often using their computers for research at home and their smartphones for in-store usage, 52 percent of consumers utilize digital coupons either frequently or occasionally. That number shoots up to 68 percent among households with kids.

Companies don't necessarily need to worry about their online sales cannibalizing in-store sales, either. According to the FMI report, engagement opportunities still exist in-store because consumers still prefer to shop in person for their fresh goods. A company can also offer different packaging sizes, flavors, and product mixes online than it does in-store to further reduce any perceived conflict.

Developing a Loyalty Club

A brand's relationship with consumers has evolved, and the big brands were the first to see it. There used to be fewer brands to compete with, and success in the food industry landscape was basically a matter who can "buy" the most consumer awareness within the market. Then, in broadcast media, the advertising options exploded from just three primary television stations to thousands of cable channels. Next came the internet, and finally, mobile devices.

With the rise of mobile devices came the rise of social media, and as discussed in the rest of this chapter, you need to be prepared to hear from people who are interacting with your brand. You should do more than just prepare for this. You should embrace it. There's a gold mine in nurturing real and direct give-and-take communications with the consumers who are buying your brand.

It's important that you join the loyalty club collective, but be ready to give something in return for your membership. Your branded website should include an option for consumers to create an account and sign up to receive coupons and branded content such as recipes, offers, and events on a regular basis. There are several secure digital coupon options out there that you can compare and contrast, but it's a good idea to start by choosing an option that connects with all or most of your core retail customers. You want to be able to make it easy for both your consumers and your retail partners. For instance, coupons.com creates secure mobile-friendly coupons for most brands, while also offering load-to-card opportunities for the supermarket loyalty programs offered by most of the country's retail stores.

One of the main functions of establishing a loyalty club is to gather consumer information. Once you get the consumer's contact information, you have the opportunity and responsibility to create an environment of loyalty and information sharing in a permission-based marketing model. Your role in the loyalty club is to provide coupons and product information such as new offerings, recipes, and purchasing locations. A consumer's role is to provide something that used to be available only to big brands with big research budgets—consumer behavior and buying data. Before social media and smartphones, this kind of data collection was all but impossible for small food brands like yours. Loyalty clubs also offer something else as well—the opportunity to interact with your customers.

Think about all the times you and your team have sat around a conference table product planning. "Do we add a new flavor and, if so, which one?" "Should we change the packaging, and if so, how?" There are probably numerous questions you would like answered before you pull the trigger and invest in a full-blown product launch. Why not ask your loyalty club members through surveys? It can help you answer some of those nagging questions, while also making your loyal customers feel like they are company insiders.

The knowledge, insights, and opinions of your loyalty club members can also be used during your presentations with buyers and retailers. Many of the buyers and retailers I spoke to found it baffling that more manufacturers didn't do this. Being able to survey your core consumers and then show buyers/retailers the specific comparative benefits of your product makes you stand out as a true expert in your category. Even if a buyer/retailer decides not to partner with you in one instance, your demonstrated commitment and expertise will create a powerful memory.

Basically, loyalty marketing enables a small, local, or regional company like yours to convert your brand equity into useful data, improved relationships, and increased profits, all at minimal cost. It's an opportunity brought on by the rise of social media, which was once unavailable to you. Taking advantage of this fact can reshape your brand and change its standing in the marketplace by enabling you to …

Compete beyond price. Attract individual consumers, their friends, and buyers/retailers to your entire brand family.

Improve your bottom line. Drive increased volume with your core customers, convert discounts and low-cost rewards into higher perceived value, and use increased profits and consumer data as a tool when you work with buyers/retailers.

Better understand your customer. Build productive relationships with consumers by analyzing your loyalty club data to better understand them as they make their way through the whole purchasing process.

Leverage your data. Cultivate beneficial partnerships with your buyers/retailers by proving that you are a category expert, increasing sales at no cost to them, and offering them a chance for data sharing and co-branded promotions.

Findings from a 2013 Nielsen study of customer loyalty revealed the fickle nature of brand loyalty. Surveying across four different food and beverage categories, the study found that only 14 to 23 percent of North Americans were completely brand-loyal, while 30 to 41 percent weren't brand-loyal at all. It leaves a sizable brand loyalty gap—one that an effective brand loyalty program can help fill.

Cultivating Brand Evangelists

If your company and its brand were a rock band and your loyalty club represented your fan base, then your brand evangelists would be your groupies. How do you convert your casual fans into groupies? By supporting a common cause and/or openly acknowledging their devotion. Nothing brings people together more like a shared vision, and there's nothing quite like letting your biggest fans spread their love through coupons that can be shared with friends or a branded event they can host for their neighbors. The 2016 Nielsen report on social media found that nearly 30 percent of heavy social media users thought it was very or somewhat important to engage with social media to show support for their favorite companies or brands. Therefore, you can be confident that the word will get out about your good thoughts and deeds.

CONCLUSION

A powerful digital presence is essential in today's business world. Throughout this book, I've talked about the evolving food industry marketplace and the different ways both consumer behavior and marketing outlets have fragmented. Developing an effective digital presence is one way to capitalize on all this change. Make sure your websites are updated and cutting-edge. Take your social media marketing program seriously so that you can lock down your most loyal fans. You don't just want to survive the digital revolution. You want to capitalize on it.

Section 5

Brand Prosperity and Long-Term Growth

Chapter 15

PUBLIC RELATIONS AND CRISIS MANAGEMENT

"Nobody wants their name dragged through the mud in the media. We've seen how many companies fail because of one time, they have an issue."

—V. L., senior buyer, 32 years' experience

I've spent the better part of this book discussing strategies to transform your company and its brand into a market leader. Your approach to public relations should be an extension of those strategies. Whether you are providing the public with a steady stream of good news that highlights the achievements of your company and its brand or dealing with an unforeseen crisis, your strategies toward public relations should be both well-planned and properly executed. I'll address these strategies in this chapter, beginning with those designed to develop and maintain a favorable presence in the public eye.

THE GOOD: STRATEGIC PUBLIC RELATIONS

Whereas proper crisis management can be seen as a good defense, an established and ongoing program of favorable public relations represents a good offense. Done correctly, it can promote your products, build your brand's reputation, and foster goodwill within your community. It also ensures that a crisis isn't the first time the public hears about you and your company. An effective underlying public relations strategy includes three basic elements: objectives, strategies, and tactics.

Objectives

You should strive to maintain a positive association between your brand name and positive things on a regular basis within your chosen region. Doing so can aid you if your goal is to transform your brand into a regional food-industry powerhouse. You probably have other, more individualized objectives, which should be tangible and achievable goals that should be articulated well.

Strategies

Your strategies should be actionable approaches to achieving your objectives. In general, your strategy is to promote your company and its brand through frequent and regular communication with your customer (the gatekeeper) and the consumer. Get your brand name out there by highlighting your significant events and achievements, including the following:

* Company expansion
* New retailer listings
* New product launches
* Ingredient or flavor changes
* Packaging alterations
* New and high-profile employee hires
* Large donations or high-profile event sponsorship

Tactics

This is where the rubber meets the road—where you implement activities to carry out each strategy. Besides keeping your good name in the news, one main idea behind a public relations plan is to maintain good relationships with media outlets. Maintaining good relationships will help you during communication with the media if/when something unfortunate happens.

Engage with your public by announcing highlights and achievements through all available media. Remember that the news releases you produce are targeted to varying parties, including both your gatekeeper and the public-at-large, and should be designed keeping each particular target in mind. Support causes, both locally and (if applicable) nationally, and formulate a formal plan for donation requests and giving so that you can budget your funds and regulate your donation announcements.

Other grassroots efforts, such as donations and charitably supporting specific causes, are important as well. Participating in local festivals and other events in the area are also activities that showcase your engagement and investment within the region.

THE BAD: CRISIS MANAGEMENT

Say your retailers and partners are happy with the performance of your products, and consumer sales are up. You've kept food safety and all the factors that it entails foremost in your mind throughout the process. There's nothing that could upset the grocery cart, right?

Wrong. According to *Food Safety Magazine*, no fewer than 764 food product recalls were issued in the United States and Canada in 2016. That number, which is based on notices issued by the U.S. Food and Drug Administration, the U.S. Department of Agriculture, and the Canadian Food Inspection Agency, marked a 22 percent surge compared to 2015.

The FDA regulates recalls for food, equipment, packaging, drugs, and medical devices for human and animal uses only. The main culprits in the 2016 recalls were undeclared allergens (305), Listeria (196), Salmonella (99), foreign matter contamination (44), and *E. coli* (31). These recalls were associated with items such as meat, dairy, nuts, seeds, and frozen vegetables, as well as glass, metal, and plastic. Among the companies impacted by the recalls were industry giants General Mills, Kellogg Company, Dole

Fresh Vegetables, Tyson Foods, Bumble Bee Foods, Nestle USA, and Hostess Brands. Clearly, no product or company is immune to these problems, and your company must be prepared to handle them.

Furthermore, product recalls are only the most obvious examples of public relations crises that your company might encounter. From controversial filling in your cookies to allegations of syringes in your sodas, there are numerous examples of distressful situations that you might not have been directly responsible for and do not involve recalls. Nonetheless, such recalls have a negative impact on sales; brand reputation; and your consumer, retailer, and shareholder relationships. Your company must be prepared to handle these situations as well.

What follows is an effective best-practices plan for crisis management, along with some analysis of the crisis management practices—both good and bad—that have been implemented during several recent product crises. A good public relations program fosters goodwill about your company, but a single slip can ruin it.

The Basics

Events beyond the control of your company can adversely affect sales; brand reputation; and consumer, retailer, and shareholder relationships. Food safety issues, customer and labor grievances, and other difficulties require a response based on a carefully planned crisis management program. This program must be designed to communicate effectively with the media and to your customers to minimize damage and maintain credibility. Faulty and inadequate communications can create a serious loss of public confidence, causing irreparable harm to your business and the value of your brand.

Here's a summary of the first steps you should take toward a suitable crisis management plan. It is designed as a preparatory device for communicating with the media—and by extension, the public—during times of distress. The following sections include the following:

* Guidelines for categorizing a situation according to its severity and whom it affects
* Advice for structuring responses to media questions
* Pointers for solidifying your chosen response and controlling public reaction in today's 24-hour news environment.

Types and Levels of Distress

To provide focused and appropriate responses, incidents are assigned a level of Class I, Class II, or Class III. Many require that different organizational areas work together as a cross-functional team to expedite resolution.

Class I (Major). Catastrophic Business Interruption: Includes death; life-threatening, or serious injury; FDA-required recall; high probability for illness or media exposure; major loss of assets; or other incidents that require cross-functional teams to resolve and/or address with utmost urgency.

Class II (Moderate): Nonlife Threatening Health or Safety Concern. Includes public relations issues; possible brand reputation damage or impact; possible impact some company assets; or other incidents that require cross-functional teams to resolve and/or address with appropriate urgency.

Class III (Minor): No Potential Threat to Life or Health. Includes public relations issues; events that might discredit brand reputation or impact company assets; or other incidents that involve limited cross-functional team interactions at address.

Note: Distress may be assessed at any level, and based on investigation, may be reclassified. For example, a team member diagnosed with an illness, such as tuberculosis, may start as a Class I distress. However, if there's no exposure to others that results in illness, this incident may be reclassified as Class III. Conversely, a Class III distress, such as an equipment fire in a store, may be reclassified as a Class I after a team member is seriously burned.

Advice for Structuring Media Responses

Not all incidents will necessarily warrant communication with the media. For example, a dispute between personnel may be considered an internal affair. However, when questioned about such matters, responses of "no comment" can be spun by the media and elevated into a story that makes the public suspicious. It's preferable in such situations to clarify that it's a matter of policy not to comment on personal matters out of the respect for the individuals involved, or if appropriate, to admit that some facts are unknown and pending further investigation.

When a Class I, II, or III incident does merit public comment, it's helpful to remember the following "Four Rs" of emergency communications. (*Note*: Not all will be applicable in every situation.)

Regret. A response should express concern that a problem has developed, even if your company is not at fault, such as in the case of a natural disaster. Expressing regret and acknowledging a problem communicates empathy or sympathy and helps an organization identify with its public.

Responsibility. Whether the cause of the crisis was the organization's fault or not, the organization should be prepared to take responsibility for solving the problem. Your actions will reinforce your words and provide a credible demonstration of your organization's commitment to doing the right thing.

Reform. Your various stakeholder audiences must know the organization is taking steps to ensure the problem will not happen again. Focus the discussion on positive future actions.

Restitution. If appropriate, detail how your organization, and perhaps the industry in general, will help those who have been affected by the issue. Restitution includes refunds, coupons, and exchanges as well as monetary compensation.

In times of crisis, strong responses to the media will do the following:

1. Express empathy, sympathy, listening, and/or compassion as an initial statement.
2. State the organization's key message.
3. Reinforce that key message by following it up with supporting information.
4. Repeat that key message.
5. State the organization's future actions.

To fulfill actions 1 through 5, consider employing the following tactics:

* Use personal pronouns such as I, we, our, and us. Indicate through body language (posture, gestures, and facial expressions) and choice of words that you share the concerns of those affected by events. Repeat keywords or phrases from their questions to let them know you are listening. Acknowledge the legitimacy of their fears and concerns.
* Limit your responses to no more than 27 words and no longer than 9 seconds (the typical "sound-bite" timed for maximum ease of use in media when reporting on a story). Use positive, constructive, solution-oriented words where appropriate, and

set key points apart with pauses, inflection, and signposts. (Signposts are words and phrases that help organize a message and show the relationship between the message's main ideas, making it much easier for the audience to understand. Examples of signposts include words like first, second, consequently, and finally, or phrases such as in addition to, for example, and in conclusion.)

* Summarize or emphasize the organization's key message.
* List the organization's specific next steps. Provide contact information for obtaining additional information, if appropriate.

Crisis Management for the Digital Age

In the digital age, everything is interconnected. Information flows faster and reaches farther than ever before. It's a blessing and a curse for organizations due to the virility of sharing videos, articles, or images. There are scenarios where you can have ample time to anticipate a crisis, and sometimes something will arise that you're not prepared for. If a crisis were to ever arise, you should be prepared for any level of media onslaught. Here are three key components to remember for navigating a crisis:

Prepare a checklist before any crisis. Always expect the unexpected. It's advised to have responses and solutions drafted for numerous scenarios. Anything can happen, from an internal incident or an employee suing you over labor rights. Without a plan, your internal chain of command may panic, and you'll lose control of not only your external communication, but your internal communication as well. Make sure your employees are all on the same page.

Be accessible. The transformation of media has led to the accessibility of individuals and information. Being able to tap into numerous channels to convey your message is a great way to get your product known. In addition, the public is also able to acknowledge your lines of two-way communication.

Answer questions to the best of your ability. Being nimble and effective is a necessity when navigating a crisis. Being forthright and transparent helps mitigate negative press as well. The truth always has a way of surfacing, and if you want to preserve your brand's integrity, always speak sincerely and honestly.

Transparency

A company's willingness to embrace the idea of full transparency has also become increasingly important in today's media-savvy culture. When a company isn't candid or deflects questions, consumers tend to think the company is hiding something. Transparency has become the new norm. Information travels like wildfire and access to said information is expected.

According to a 2015 analysis by The Hartman Group, transparency conveys accountability and authenticity, and it can be a potent strategic tool to build consumer trust and loyalty in the following ways:

* Transparency speaks to a consumer's desire for connectedness and control in an increasingly complex and competitive consumer landscape.
* Transparency reveals product quality and company integrity.
* Transparency creates a bond that transforms a typical transaction into a brand relationship.
* Transparency enables consumers to make intentional choices based on easy access to relevant and truthful information about products, ingredients, sourcing, and business practices.

Your company should always remember that its consumers are the most sophisticated, educated, and connected in history. Transparency can be used as a tool to build your business and your brand, while a lack of transparency can potentially destroy it.

THE GOOD, THE BAD, AND THE *E. COLI*

Perhaps the best indicator that a crisis has been managed well is that it has been forgotten altogether. The public can't recall that recall. Nobody important is talking about that PR scandal. Even Google has buried your so-called crisis under a mountain of information that is, at most, tangentially related to your product.

Many crises that have been successfully managed have been handled using the principles explained earlier in this chapter. By implementing the appropriate combination of the Four Rs—regret, responsibility, reform, and restitution—and remaining diligent in that implementation, the crisis has been addressed and contained in a way that minimizes damage.

Following are a few prominent examples of good crisis management within the food industry, as well as one example of crisis management gone wrong. There were many to choose from, both good and bad, but you can believe that the bad ones were much easier to find. Viewing each of these crises through the lens of the Four Rs should reveal why each situation resulted as it did.

The Good: Tylenol and Disaster

This example is perhaps the mother of all crisis management success stories. In 1982, seven Chicago-area people died after ingesting doses of the Johnson & Johnson pain reliever Tylenol, which had been laced with the deadly poison potassium cyanide. The poisonings resulted in a nationwide consumer scare, and Johnson & Johnson's response to the scare set the guidelines on effective public relations and crisis management.

Johnson & Johnson responded swiftly. First, the company went public via both print and television media outlets, expressing regret and instructing the public to cease all use of Tylenol. Johnson & Johnson then pulled $100 million worth of Tylenol off the shelves and halted all production and advertising of the product. It also got involved with law enforcement authorities and the FDA as they searched for the killer, even offering a $100,000 reward for clues leading to the capture.

While the killer was never caught, Johnson & Johnson did rebound from the crisis. The company reintroduced Tylenol with tamper-resistant packaging, which now an industry standard, and offered $2.50-off coupons on the new product. Both the media and consumers appreciated the actions Johnson & Johnson took during the crisis, so the company was generally viewed in a good light and the Tylenol brand recovered.

Tylenol's success story went well beyond simple regret. Johnson & Johnson took responsibility for the crisis even though it was not at fault. The company also embraced reform by introducing safer packaging and made restitution by offering steep discounts on the new product through coupons.

The Good: Odwalla and *E. coli*

In 1996, Odwalla Foods encountered and overcame a significant crisis when it was still an upstart juice company. The issue arose when health officials in the state of Washington confirmed a link between a local *E. coli* outbreak and Odwalla's fresh unpasteurized apple juice. One child died and more than 60 other people were sickened as a result of this outbreak, and more than 20 lawsuits were filed.

The company responded by recalling all Odwalla products containing apple or carrot juice, at a cost of approximately $6.5 million. Odwalla's CEO then took public responsibility for the episode and promised to pay all medical costs for those impacted by the outbreak. The company also held daily press briefings with updates on the crisis and used newspaper ads and a new website to explain the situation. Odwalla suffered through significant loss in revenue and market share, but they relaunched their apple juice line two months later. In 2001, Coca-Cola bought Odwalla for $186 million.

Odwalla followed the Four Rs, were transparent in their message, and employed of all available media. Odwalla's handling of the *E. coli* ordeal serves as another textbook example of good crisis management.

The Good: Diet Pepsi, Oreo Cookies, and Public Perception

At different times, PepsiCo and Kraft Foods both faced potential public relations crises that never involved product recalls, but nevertheless threatened to negatively impact their public standing. Both companies responded with actions that went beyond a simple press release and quickly resolved their issues.

In 1993, PepsiCo was faced with a crisis after a syringe was allegedly found in a can of Diet Pepsi in the state Washington. Within a week, more than 50 reports of Diet Pepsi can tampering sprung up across the country. PepsiCo and the FDA were confident that these reports were fabrications, but the hoax was gaining steam in the public-at-large.

PepsiCo responded aggressively in defending itself against the accusations. Their North American CEO appeared on several major news stations armed with the explicit support of the FDA as well as visual evidence of the bogus reports and their meticulous soda canning process. The rumors fizzled out within two weeks, and Diet Pepsi sales recovered within a month.

Kraft Foods found itself with a potential crisis in 2013, when the company introduced a specialty rainbow variety of its Oreo cookies in support of Gay Pride Month. This move involved nothing more than food coloring and cookie filling. However, controversy loomed when many consumers with strong feelings about the issue responded to the rainbow cookies with criticism and backlash.

Using social media, Kraft teamed up with its loyal consumer base to avert the crisis. After an overwhelming number of consumers took to social media in defense of the company, Kraft further contained the issue by responding to the unhappy parties. The crisis did not escalate any further.

PepsiCo and Kraft Foods didn't necessarily have to utilize the Four Rs principles because neither were dealing with product recalls. Still, both companies did follow proper protocol by responding quickly and decisively, displaying transparency and taking advantage of all media available to them.

The Bad: Dole Salads and Listeria

A 2016 recall by Dole Fresh Vegetables serves as a prime example of a case of seemingly good crisis management gone bad. In January 2016, Dole recalled the branded and private label-packaged salads that had been processed at its Springfield, Ohio, plant due to the possibility of Listeria contamination. Dole, which also temporarily suspended production at the plant due to the recall, promptly released a statement that included an apology, a promise to address the issue, a reminder of its commitment to food safety, and an explicit pledge to remain transparent throughout the ordeal. The company appeared to be utilizing all the principles of good crisis management.

Just three months later, however, *Food Safety News* published information culled from FDA inspection reports that revealed a history of positive Listeria results and inaction at the Springfield plant. As reported in *Food Safety News* and the FDA reports, Dole was aware of the Listeria contamination at the plant as early as July 2014, but they didn't shut down operations until the news went public in January 2016. By then, at least 33 people had fallen ill and four had died from the Listeria strain that was found at the Springfield plant. This time, when Dole was forced to address the issue a second time, its statement mentioned not only the FDA but also the U.S. Department of Justice as well.

Dole's handling of the 2016 Listeria crisis failed in several ways. Even though it expressed regret and concern again in its second statement, Dole's words were likely viewed untrustworthy. The actual acceptance of responsibility and commitment to reform were absent until both actions were imposed by outside authorities. Transparency simply didn't exist. Ultimately, the two public statements began to appear side by side at the top of the first page in even the simplest of Google searches.

CONCLUSION

A thorough plan, one that's both strategic and all-encompassing, is the cornerstone of effective public relations. This plan begins with a program of regular media and public interaction that showcases activities and achievements that help define your company, increase brand awareness within your community, and develop good media relations. When a crisis occurs, you must be prepared for it, choose the correct responses, and react both quickly and effectively. How you plan and implement your public relations strategy may ultimately determine the future success or failure of your brand.

Chapter 16

STRATEGIC PRODUCT DEVELOPMENT

> *"A good supplier, we felt, was a good, forward-thinking supplier—one that was able to stay ahead of the curve."*
>
> —J. C., senior buyer, 26 years' experience

"The greatest thing since sliced bread." This cliché is used often to describe unparalleled excellence in just about any endeavor, and most people use it offhandedly. You, however, are not most people. In fact, as a manufacturer and/or supplier of food products, you are in fact in a unique position. You, your company, and its brand can become the greatest thing since sliced bread if you embrace innovation and apply the principles of strategic product development.

FIRST TO MARKET: INNOVATION THAT WINS

For every innovation that arrives first to market by one forward-thinking company, there are hundreds of companies with "me-too" brands or product lines who are saying, "if only we had thought of that." Sliced bread, which was introduced to consumers in 1928, is widely regarded as the food industry's most significant innovation of the modern age. However, there are many more, but only some were sparked by inventions like the bread-slicing machine. Who in the food industry wouldn't want to be the best thing since frozen food? The list is endless. There are first-to-market innovations, such as Jell-O, which are driven almost solely by repurposing an existing item and marketing it well. There are innovations driven by advances in packaging, such as TV dinners, bagged salads, and single-serve coffee pods. In addition, there are also those driven by trends in consumer preferences, such as organic foods, fat-free foods, and 100-calorie servings.

This leads us to the big question—one that the retail buyers interviewed for this book showed a keen interest in: How can local or regional brands be first to market when large national brands have seemingly inexhaustible resources for research and development?

As mentioned in Chapter 2, Rabobank published a report in 2015 stating that many of America's largest food and beverage companies were losing sales because of evolving and shifting consumer preferences. Those preferences were trending toward locally produced, transparent, natural, and/or organic practices, as well as community-minded corporate responsibility values. Furthermore, Big Food was losing their market share to local or smaller brands that were more flexible, responsive, and nimble by nature. Comparatively speaking, large food companies are slow to market and tend to favor a protective product development philosophy that tweaks the status quo of their flagship money-making brands with minor and safe upgrades. Retail buyers are, therefore, looking toward small to mid-sized food companies that are better positioned to launch disruptive and/or innovative products in the market.

Commit to Win

Most successful new products are the result of innovation, which can only come after a manufacturer/supplier has become an expert in their category. An expert must know not only the goals of his or her own company, but also the needs of their gate-keeping retailer and the desires of their end-line consumers. Furthermore, this expert must know how to follow through by presenting his or her product properly and validating their proposal with real-world test results.

These factors are part of strategic product development, which can be defined as the development of products with new or different characteristics that offer new or additional benefits to the customer. Product development (strategic or otherwise) can be viewed as expensive and time consuming, which may lead to it being dismissed or ignored altogether by a company focused on sales and delivery. That's all well and good, if you want to be a "me-too" brand or product line. Simply put, strategic product development can make you an expert among experts and place your brand's products at the forefront of their category. We have broken our proven method of strategic product management into three distinct areas: research, ideation, and validation.

Research

While calling it "research" may sound a bit clinical, you are researching when you when develop and maintain continuous processes to keep abreast of everything from global macro trends to evolving consumer food preferences to supermarket-selling trends. All of this information is vital to have if you want to be perceived as an expert in your category.

Regardless of what it's called, anything related to research and product development should begin with the end consumer, followed by the gatekeepers—your retailers and category managers (your retail grocer customers)—and finally, your particular product category parameters. In other words, it must fit into the category and the supermarket's planogram. Let's start here: always begin by identifying and understanding the end user.

IDENTIFY YOUR "IDEAL" CONSUMER
It's a Mom-Centric World (We Just Live in It)

In today's world, your target demographic almost always begins and ends with mom. In the 2011 book, *Tuning into Mom*, authors Michal Clements and Teri Lucie Thompson formally summarize close to a decade of articles, trend reports, and research on America's most powerful consumer—mom. American mothers oversee an estimated $2.45 trillion in direct spending and significantly influence the spending habits of other consumers in their households. Recent research from Food Marketing Institute in the 2016 U.S. Grocery Shopping Trends report shows that dad is gaining significance, especially in younger millennial families and those that share shopping duties (known as *co-shopping*). Still, mothers ultimately make most of the shopping decisions. Even in multi-person households where spouses said they co-shopped, women were the primary shoppers 69 percent of the time.

Attitudes, Perceptions, Lifestyle, and Life Stages

One way to further narrow the focus on your target audience is to understand their psychographic makeup (attitudes and perceptions). Let's continue to use mom as the prime example here. How old is mom when she's buying most of your products? How old are her kids? What are her personality traits, interests, and values? What is she searching for on Pinterest or talking about on Facebook? If she's a young and idealistic mother, she might prefer healthy dietary alternatives for her family. A busy, multi-tasking, working mother might come to the realization that she might as well give in and feed her kids mac and cheese. Which mom do you want to sell your product to?

Demographics: The Segment of Your Ideal Consumer

Gender, age, income level, and the geographic location of your target demographic are also important factors to consider as you familiarize yourself with your ideal consumer. According to the 2015 Deloitte report cited in Chapter 2, wealthier consumers tend to be more willing to pay a higher price for their groceries, and are therefore more likely to opt for the trendier and more expensive all-natural, organic, and/or non-GMO products. In addition, there are also the millions of other Americans who require options when they go to the store to pick up their everyday box of cereal.

Your Consumer's Buying Behavior

There are several questions you need to ask yourself when determining your consumer's buying behavior. Is your food product a destination purchase—one that consumers go to the store specifically to buy? Or is it an occasionally on-the-weekly-menu product? When the consumer shops the planogram in your category, what factors into their product selection and purchase—price, brand, package, shelf placement, or coupons? Ultimately, you must determine the consumer's selection and purchasing processes and average spending. Consider taking a field trip to the store, and watch people as they shop. You'll find out a lot from an informal store intercept if you can find a willing retail partner with which to work. Your research will pay off handsomely as you develop your expert status.

Tracking and Leveraging Food Trends

As mentioned earlier, the packaged food industry is driven by complex and ever-changing consumer tastes. It's vital that you remain dialed into current and future trends, especially as a small- to mid-sized food brand. Luckily, according to Plunkett Research, Ltd., the global food and beverage industry in 2016 was roughly an $8.0 trillion market. You can rest assured that credible and informative trend reports are plentiful and easy accessible.

Here are a few of our top go-to resources for food trends research and industry reports:

* Food Marketing Institute (FMI)
* Deloitte
* Grocery Manufacturers Association
* Industry publications such as *Supermarket News*, *Progressive Grocer*, *Food Business News*, *Food Processing*, and many more specifically reporting on your category
* Your Industry Association (e.g., the National Pork Council, the National Dairy Council, etc.

Keeping in tune with trends is crucial to the strategic development process. As you read this, some of the current growing consumer trends are squarely focused around healthy eating, including natural, organic, and non-GMO products, preferences for locally raised and produced items, meal solutions, online ordering and curbside service, and packaging variations. The question is, how will you leverage one or more of these to gain an edge, specifically additional SKUs in the marketplace? It starts with knowing who your first sale is to, and that's your gatekeepers.

IDENTIFY THE GATEKEEPER(S)
Buyer Needs and Preferences

Whether it's a retail buyer, a category manager, or the vice president of procurement within your category, the retail gatekeeper is the decision-maker in your food world. As a small- to mid-sized regional food brand, you have a unique opportunity to partner with grocery chains of all sizes by understanding what the buyer is looking for in a vendor partner.

Interviews and surveys conducted with retailers for this book indicated that suppliers often overlook this factor. Some retailers focus on batch or package size, lead time, and shrinkage, while others concentrate on fill rate, presentation windows, and margin requirements. Every one of them considers food safety a top concern. Retailers are busy people who feel like they get busier every day. There are several questions that you should ask them, most of which lead to increased focus and more efficient interactions with you. However, the retailers I talked to claim that not enough suppliers ask even the most basic of questions, "What do you need?" Even fewer suppliers ask that question and follow through on it with research, analysis, and an answer.

IN THEIR OWN WORDS:
Questions Our Retailers Wish More Suppliers Would Ask

> *"What are other items that they can develop or produce for the retailer? Also, how can we partner with you to grow all our sales going forward? I think that sometimes questions like that don't get asked or discussed because everybody's focused on today, today, today and whatever items are being worked on now. We must maintain and work on everyday business, but how do we continue to grow? And what's the next trick?"*
>
> —J. B., senior buyer, 25 years' experience

> *"Find out what your buyer's objectives are. What are his goals? Then analyze, even if it takes a month. Go back and analyze everything and say, okay, how can we help him achieve his goals and his objectives?"*
>
> —P. L., senior buyer, 25 years' experience

> "A lot of times (suppliers) will come in with their set agenda and give you their canned speech of what they have and not even ask, 'What are you looking for?' So, 'What's each retailer looking for?' can really narrow that down so that, when they come in for that meeting, they're really prepared."
>
> —W. A., senior buyer, 25 years' experience

Your Category: Stepping Stone or Career Stop?

Where your particular gatekeepers stand in their career paths is also an important factor to consider. Depending on the size and set-up of their company as well as their category, the gatekeepers you work with may not be the same person throughout your working relationship with that company. While some gatekeepers keep the same job for years, many of them change jobs often as they navigate their career paths. This is important to know because if your gatekeeper frequently changes, you might find yourself proving your expertise in your category more frequently.

IDENTIFY THE CATEGORY PARAMETERS
Understand the Playing Field

This is where you begin to study your product's positioning within its planogram. In order to determine who your competition is, regular store checks are a must. You must leave these checks with a complete list of manufacturers, product lines and names, features, and price points—anything that helps you determine how you might differentiate your product from the others. Then, after taking a few photos and jotting down some notes at the store, you must analyze the results of your store checks. Planogram arrangements differ from location to location, store type to store type, and you need to understand them all. Who are all the players in your planogram? What is your share of that?

Category Size

If you are committed to growing your market share, we recommend regularly buying category and geo-specific IRI and Nielsen reports. These reports will enable you to work from a foundation of facts, starting with your regional and overall category size, while also verifying your competitive market share. In turn, combining all of this information with the rest you gleaned from your store visits will help you strategically determine who the heavy hitters are and who might be ripe for the picking. Once you have identified the products that fall into the latter category, it's your job to displace them.

Ideation

If research is homework, then ideation is as close as you'll come to recess. By now, you fully understand the end user, the gatekeeper, and your category. It's up to you to next determine what is missing or can be displaced within that category and develop a product to occupy that position. To do so, you need to engage in the ideation process, and then engage in controlled creative brainstorming, perhaps through what is called a *blue-sky session* where the team is encouraged to come up with original or creative ideas before they must be grounded by convention and reality.

Engage in the Ideation Process

To begin, identify your main objective ("We want to fill Gap A") and formulate the core question ("What can we do to fill Gap A?"). Next, invite the right people into the process, including representatives from the manufacturing; distribution; and the creative, research, and development departments. Identify your customers, decision-makers, and stakeholders, and invite them, too, because they are the ones who'll have final say on whether a product is made. Finally, assign a facilitator to oversee the entire proceedings.

Engage in a Creative Brainstorming/Blue Sky Session

To keep the ideation process organized, brainstorming sessions must be scheduled so that an official agenda can be set and all interested parties can take part. Within these sessions, every idea is valid and ripe for tweaking. Start with an uninterrupted period of idea development, using positive phrases like, "yes, and…" "great, can we add…" to build and develop each idea—no matter how crazy—into a proposed end product. Then, embark on a rigorous concept review of each proposed product, factoring in the opinions of each interested party before settling on a real-product takeaway. Finally, discuss the marketing and sales of that product.

Validation

Both my team and the retail buyers we interviewed saw this as an area of strategic product development that is often overlooked. Having done all the homework and brainstormed your way to a product that can corner the market, you likely think you're ready to take the food world by storm. Yet, what do the end users think? Ultimately, this is arguably the most important factor to your retailer. Therefore, you must consider if your product will really sell. Validate the quality of your product and please your retailer by testing all your new ideas with real-world experiences and feedback.

Test New Ideas

Obtain real-world consumer input by conducting focus groups for all new product ideas, with your goal of seeing the products from the consumer's viewpoint. If possible, conduct focus group sessions in a controlled environment where you can observe and record the behavior of the test subjects. Test for every new aspect of your product, including everything from flavoring to packaging. Use the results from this testing to make any critical or subtle product or communication changes before too much time, effort, and money has been invested. This part of the process lends credibility and offers support to the new product as you introduce it to the gatekeepers.

Feedback Tools

There are ways beyond focus-group testing that you can receive consumer feedback, including email surveys and responses from members of your company's loyalty club. What ideas do your proven fans have about this (and other possible future) products? In the end, what you want to learn from consumer feedback is how the target market at-large is likely to view the product. Also, you're your product's price elasticity to determine your consumers' sensitivity to price change. The price of your product and where it falls within its category upon release is often a make-or-break issue.

Bringing Your Product to Market

There are several aspects to this stage of product development, but the initial introduction of your product to the market is the most important factor for our purposes here.

The marketing team—whether you use your in-house marketing team, hire a firm like NewPoint, or as we see often, a combination of these resources—will typically create a launch program that includes everything required to sell the product from developing presentations outlining the research, trends, and data, used to develop the product; to packaging comps, sell sheets, and webpages showcasing features and benefits; and finally to press releases and a tradeshow program to properly introduce the product to the world. In short, introduce your new product to the world properly.

CONCLUSION

The food world, like any other industry, thrives on innovation. Your customer—the gatekeeper—expects it and your gatekeepers' customers crave it. Through strategic product development, you, your company, and your brand can deliver innovation. However, successful development takes more than simply knowing your product. You must become a true expert in your category and be able to see your vision via the processes of research, ideation, and validation. Only then will you have a chance at becoming the best thing since sliced bread.

ACKNOWLEDGEMENTS

I'd like to thank the following people for their help with this book.
Our clients who trust me and my team with their vision, goals and budgets to drive growth for their brands.
I'd like to thank the retail buyers and category managers who were interviewed and surveyed for this book.
To Vince Ligas, for his valuable consultation and insights drawn from 40+ years in retail food category management, sourcing and buying.
My fellow executives at Warren Industries—JP Clauson, Paul House, Guy Thomas and Debra Neiferd for helping a marketing guy bridge the gap between marketing and manufacturing operations, sourcing, finance, retail sales and HR; President Barrie Simpson for showing us all how to nurture a team's individual strengths to create the shared vision required to achieve category leadership.
The sharp and ever-opinionated team at NewPoint starting with Stephanie Bossung, Brant Baumann and Ashley Morgan who provided notes and direction, Kristy Blair, for her eagle eye, Mitchell Terpstra, Ryan Klimt and Karen Gray who provided support related to their expertise and Stuart Bilan who was instrumental in providing research and notes.
And for their support, my family starting with my parents Mary and Joe and sisters Traci and Christina. For their sense of humor and perspective on today's culture, my sons Tyler and Charlie, both studying at Indiana University.
Finally, my awesome wife Cindy, who inspires me every day with her love, strength and wit. She was my biggest cheerleader on this project and was incredibly generous with her time and advice along the way.
Special thanks go to Aaron Martin. His ability to follow my multiple outlines and sift through the research, interviews and notes to develop cohesive, organized chapters were critical in helping me write this book.

INDEX

A

advertising 7, 9, 17, 18, **38-40**, 42, 43, 49, 55, 64, 72, 73, 75, 94, 115-118, 136, 140, 143-145, 152, 163, 178
allegations 171
allergens 170
all-natural 22, 186
all-organic 21
amplification 28
analytics 11, 62, 134

B

best-practices 171
big-brand 73
billboard 76, 83, 90, **116**, 152, 156
blind-taste 39
blue-sky 190
boomers 13
boosted 95
boosts 57
brainstorming 190, 191
brand 2-10, 17, 19, 20, 22, 23, 29-31, 35, **37-48**, 50, 52, 54, 56, 58-60, 62, 64-66, 68, 69, 71-104, 106-121, 124-161, 163-165, 167-172, 174, 176-178, 180-182, 184, 186-188, 190, 192, 193
brand activation 136-140
brand-eat-brand 79

branded visual identity 6
branding **37-40**, 42, 45, 72, 73, 82, 84, 86
brand-integrated 46
brand message 79
brand position **77-79**
brand-tactical 44, 46
buyer 2, 3, 5, 7, 8, 19, 20, **24-31**, 33, 59, 61, 67, 68, 88, 110, 136, 140, 143, 149, 153, 154, 164, 168, 182, 187-189
buying behavior 186

C

call-to-action 116, 136
campaigns 6, 40, 41, 46, 75, 76, **112-126**, 130, 135
category parameters 189
clean labeling 104-105
co-branded 126, 143, 165
collaborative 42
community-minded 183
complaint 158
complaints 7, 25, 161
consumer-based 107
consumer-driven 8, 67
coupons 94, 95, 116, 126, 135, **141**, 142, 152, 162, 163, 165, 174, 178, 186
crisis management 174
customer service 161

D

demographics 8, 64, 68, 88, 97, 118, 131, **186**
demos **117**, 126, 152
difference-maker 98
differentiation 5, 6, 29, 77, 87, 100, 131, **132**, 138
digital 6-9, 13, 15, 25, 38, 42, 46, 83, 90, 95, 112-115, 117, 118, 125, 126, 132, 134, 135, 142, 145, 146, 152, **154-159**, 161-163, 165, 166, 175
Direct-mail 142
direct-to-consumer 14
disruptive 183

E

earth-friendly 105
entrepreneur 23, 91
entrepreneurial 8, 19, 65
evangelists 7, 165
extension 42, 153, 168, 172

F

Facebook 29, 51, 76, 93, 113, 134, 146, 152, **157-160**, 185
facings 154
FDA-required 172
first-to-market 26, 182
focus-groups 64, 192
food-buying 88, 103

G

gatekeeper 2, 30, 68, 169, 170, **187-193**
generic 73, 74, 134, 149
geo-specific 190
gluten-free 21
grassroots 7, 18, 28, 46, 117, 134, 135, 145-147, **151-152**, 170
ground-zero 35

H

high-profile 129, 169
high-tech 9
high-traffic 116
home-delivered 66

I

ideation 64, 184, **190-191**, 193
identity 6, 46, **83-91**, 93-97, 107, 112, 117, 130-132, 134, 146
impressions 107, 130, 134
innovate 19, 30, 67
innovation 7, 63, 109, 135, **182-183**, 193
Instagram **92-93**, 115, 152
in-store 126, 140, 141, 147, 152, 162
internet 79, 87, 113, 128, 145, 156, 163
internet-based 145

K

keyword 114
keywords 115, 174

L

label 2, 25, 32, 46, 102-106
logos 83, 85, 89, 90, 99
loyalty club 162-165

M

marketplaces 152
market-ready 38
markets 8, 35, 57, 146, 151
media-savvy 176
mid-aisle 94
millennials **8-9**, 12, 13, 16, 18, 89, 132, 159, 162
mobile 8, 13, 114, 119, **133**, 141, 163
mobile-friendly 163

N

name-brand 5
non-GMO 68, 186, 187
nutrition facts labeling 102-103

O

off-brand 74
optimization 114, 115

organic 20, 21, 66, 68, 77-79, 183, 186, 187
organics 32, 33

P

package 7, 29, 62, 92, 97, 99-101, 103, 107, 108, 186, 188
packaging 5, 6, 21, 22, 29, 32, 39, 46, 48, 49, 52, 63, 64, 66, 73, 76, 83, 85, 86, 90, 93, 97-101, 103, 105-111, 135, 143, 162, 164, 169, 170, 178, 182, 187, 192
Pinterest 155, 185
planogram (POG) **27-29**, 31, 63, 184, 186, 189
point-of-purchase 83, **94**, 140, 145, 152
point-of-sale 128
positioned 116, 128, 129, 183
positioning 4, 40, 43, 45, 64, 76-80, 91, 94, 131, 139, 156, 189
psychographic 144, 185
psychographics 64, 88, 97, 131
public relations 168-169

Q

qualitative 44, 45, 60, 61, 63-65, 68
quantitative 44, 45, 60, 61, 63, 68

R

Rabobank 11, 12, 15, 183

recall 172, 177, 180
recalls 7, 170, 171, 179, 180
regional brand powerhouse 7
regulations 3, 102
restocking 25

S

safety 3, 6, 13, 32, 33, 98, 100, 101, 107, 110, 170-172, 180, 181, 188
scalability 138
scalable 42, 141, 142
sell-through 125, 139, 140, 153
shopper marketing 63, 83, **94**
shrinkage 28, 188
signage 86
SKU 56, 63, 66, 69, 187,
slogan 79, 81
small-batch 66
smartphone 157, 159
Snapchat 93
social media 8, 113, **146-147**
social media marketing 155-160
sponsorship 140, 169
start-up 9
strategic 5, 7, 42, 51, **54-58**, 114, 115, 124, 135, 146, 147, 156, 161, 168, 176, **181-189**, 191, 193
store checks 63
style guide 92
surveys 64

T

tampering 100-101
Tasty food videos 93
transparency 3, **13-18**, 104, 105, **176-177**, 180, 181
trend 6, **16**, 20, 25, 29, 32, 52, 61, 66-69, 104, 128, 135, **186-187**
tweet 76, 146, **155**
Twitter **113**, 134, 152, 156, 157, 159, 161

U

user-generated 114

V

value proposition 82

W

website 21, 22, 48, 49, 62, 102, 106, **113-115**, 133, 134, 162, 163, 179
well-positioned 25

CPSIA information can be obtained
at www.ICGtesting.com
Printed in the USA
BVHW030616011118
531857BV00003B/566/P